TRAVELLERS

BERLIN

By
CHRIS AND MELANIE RICE

Written by Chris and Melanie Rice, updated by Tom Bross
Original photography by Antony Souter and Christopher Holt,
updated photography by Tom Bross

Published by Thomas Cook Publishing
A division of Thomas Cook Tour Operations Limited.
Company registration no. 1450464 England
The Thomas Cook Business Park, Unit 9, Coningsby Road,
Peterborough PE3 8SB, United Kingdom
Email: books@thomascook.com, Tel: + 44 (0) 1733 416477
www.thomascookpublishing.com

Produced by Cambridge Publishing Management Limited
Burr Elm Court, Main Street, Caldecote CB23 7NU

ISBN: 978-1-84157-932-0

Series Editor: Maisie Fitzpatrick
Production/DTP: Steven Collins

Printed and bound in Italy by Printer Trento

Cover photography: Front: © Ripani Massimo/SIME-4Corners Images; © Photoshot (World Pictures); © Amantini Stefano/4Corners Images; Back: © Ripani Massimo/SIME-4Corners Images; © Photoshot/mauritius images

The paper used for this book has been independently certified as having been sourced from well-managed forests and recycled wood or fibre according to the rules of the Forest Stewardship Council.
This book has been printed and bound in Italy by Printer Trento S.r.l., an FSC certified company for printing books on FSC mixed paper in compliance with the chain of custody and on products labelling standards.

Contents

KEY TO MAPS

- ✈ Airport
- A100 Road number
- S S-Bahn
- U U-Bahn
- ★ Start of walk/tour

Introduction

Berlin has rushed headlong through the past millennium hardly daring to draw breath. The sprawling city, capital of one of the largest countries in Europe, and of a nation challenged and reinvigorated by unification, also has a past at times tragic, at times disturbing, but always fascinating.

Berliners are proud of the sheer size and diversity of their city. Their ancestors in the 19th century looked on in amazement as the boundaries extended ever outward and the population doubled and re-doubled from one generation to the next. Its writers dubbed Berlin a *Grossstadt* (great city) but also a *Weltstadt* (world city) – with connotations of municipal magnificence and civic grandeur, a place where everything was available on a superlative scale, and where no one was disappointed. The description rings true even today.

Charlottenburg Palace

It was in the 19th century, too, that Berlin discovered its reverence for the civilisations of the past. Modern Berlin still benefits from that superb cultural inheritance in its world-class museums. Its magnificent architectural heritage ranges from the Baroque splendour of the Forum Fredericianum to the neoclassical majesty of Schinkel's Schauspielhaus; from the great palaces

THOMAS COOK'S BERLIN

Thomas Cook first advertised trips to Berlin in 1880. In 1896 Cooks was appointed Official International Tourist Agents to the Berlin Exhibition, offering a first-class return fare to Berlin via Harwich and Hamburg for £3 4s 2d. It remained a popular destination and the first Cooks representative office opened there in 1906 at Weltreisebüro Union.

Museum Island, home to many of Berlin's treasures

built by the Hohenzollerns at Sanssouci and Charlottenburg to the modern architecture of the world-renowned Bauhaus school.

Yet there is more to Berlin than culture. The neighbourhood of the Kurfürstendamm is a shopper's paradise: KaDeWe, the largest department store in Europe, is itself a tourist sight. No other continental city has such an abundance of green spaces. A bus ride away from the Ku'damm is the Grunewald forest and the Wannsee, with its yachting marinas and beaches. To the east is the Müggelsee, quieter nowadays and less commercialised, but no less beautiful.

Above all, Berlin is its people – enterprising and energetic, irreverent, with a rich vein of sardonic humour, generous, kind-hearted, tolerant and fun.

The city

Berlin lies on a vast lowland plain in northeastern Germany, which accounts for the almost total absence of hills – nowhere is higher than about 70m (230ft) above sea level. The city was founded at the lowest crossing point of the Spree. The sandy terrain, punctuated by rivulets, bogs and channels, continues to affect the foundations of buildings to this day.

However, the soil also accounts for the proliferation of woodland which, despite having been cleared repeatedly over the centuries, continues to be a source of relaxation and enjoyment for Berliners. Today there are about 3.5 million Berliners, and the city is still Germany's largest, extending over an area of about 1,000sq km (386sq miles), more than one-third of which consists of forests, fields and lakes.

Climate

Officially Berlin has a continental climate, but the cold winters one would expect at this latitude, brought in by the Siberian blast from the east, are modified by warmer fronts emanating from Western Europe. Summers can be fresh and sunny, but are not usually very hot. Rainfall is substantial, but is distributed fairly evenly throughout the year.

Economy

Berlin's industrial base is concentrated in the eastern half of the city, where food processing and consumer industries exist alongside large-scale engineering plants. The economy in the West still suffers from a long-standing dependence on massive American and later West German investment, a consequence of its peculiar geographical and political isolation.

Since reunification, the situation in Berlin mirrors the rest of the country, the main problem being how to integrate two such disparate economies. Industry in the East still suffers from outmoded technology and low productivity and is struggling to compete. High unemployment is another unwelcome outcome of exposure to the chill winds of market capitalism. The policy of the united German government, put crudely, is to subsidise the East with grants, low-interest loans and tax incentives – a fearfully expensive solution which is already facing stiff opposition from many quarters.

Pollution

Berlin's reputation for invigorating air, the famous *Berliner Luft*, is being challenged by pollution. The sources are easily identifiable – factories producing sulphur dioxide and car and bus emissions of nitrogen oxide. Some of the culprits have been exposed and been taken to task.

Cleaning up is now a priority. Recycling of all waste products, long practised in the West, is now happening in the East. Restrictions are being introduced on the use of brown lignite coal as a source of energy. Car-owners are being urged to buy lead-free petrol and to use the city's first-rate public transport system whenever possible. But because East Germany had merely an emergent environmental policy, it took at least five years after reunification to clean up. Now East–West standards are comparable.

Funkturm and International Congress Centre

History

1307 The twin communities of Berlin and Cölln are brought under one administration.

1417 Frederick of Hohenzollern is proclaimed Elector Frederick I.

1443 Frederick II ('Irontooth') builds the first Berlin Schloss (or Castle).

1618–48 The Thirty Years' War; Berlin is occupied by Austrian and Swedish forces. The population is halved to about 6,000.

1640–88 Frederick William I, the 'Great Elector', revives the fortunes of Berlin.

1688 Accession of Elector Frederick III.

1701 The Elector crowns himself King Frederick I of Prussia.

1713–40 Frederick William I of Prussia, the 'Soldier King', turns Potsdam into a garrison town and Berlin into a barracks.

1740 Accession of Frederick the Great. Berlin is embellished but retains its military character.

1756–63 Seven Years' War. Berlin is occupied by Austrian troops in 1757 and again by Russians in 1760.

1788 Carl Gotthard Langhans designs the Brandenburg Gate as an arch of peace.

1806 Frederick William III is defeated at Jena. Napoleon enters Berlin.

1810 Humboldt University founded.

1837 The Industrial Revolution gets underway with the founding of August Borsig's locomotive works in Kreuzberg.

1848 Barricades are set up by rioting crowds. Frederick William IV promises free elections but subsequently goes back on his promise.

1862 William I appoints Bismarck Minister-President of Prussia.

1871 France's defeat in the Franco-Prussian War. Berlin declared capital of a unified Germany.

1888	Kaiser William II becomes ruler of Germany.
1918	World War I ends. The Kaiser abdicates and a German Republic is proclaimed.
1920	Eight towns and 59 villages are merged to create Greater Berlin.
1933	Hitler becomes Chancellor of Germany.
1936	Berlin hosts the Olympic Games.
1938	*Reichskristallnacht* (the night of broken glass).
1939–45	World War II.
1945	Berlin falls. Under Allied occupation, it is divided into four sectors.
1948–9	The Berlin Airlift. Germany is divided into the Federal Republic (West) and the German Democratic Republic (East).
1961	The Berlin Wall is built.
1989	The collapse of Communism in East Berlin and the opening of the Wall.
1990	The Wall comes down.
1991	The German parliament votes to move the site of the government to Berlin.
1999	September 1 sees both the government and Deutscher Bundestag settled in Berlin.
2001	Berlin's first openly gay mayor Klaus Wowereit is elected.
2005	Angela Merkel becomes first female Chancellor.
2006	Berlin's Olympic Stadium hosts football's World Cup championship matches. Construction of Berlin's multi-level, Spree-riverside *Hauptbahnhof* (main railway station) completed.
2007	One hundredth anniversaries of west-side Berlin's KaDeWe department store and Kempinski's Adlon Hotel. Sixtieth anniversary of the Marshall Plan. Germany's largest synagogue, on Rykestrasse, rededicated. Chancellor Merkel's one-year presidency of the European Council.
2008	Fifth Berlin Contemporary Art Biennale (April to June). State elections in Bavaria, Hesse and Lower Saxony.

The Brandenburg Gate

For more than 200 years the fortunes of the Brandenburger Tor (Brandenburg Gate) have been inseparably bound up with those of the German people. Designed in 1788 by Carl Gotthard Langhans in neoclassical style, it was intended as a Gateway to Peace. The addition by Schadow of the goddess Viktoria driving her chariot, the Quadriga, four years later when Prussia was at war with France, was designed to reinforce the vision of peace triumphant. When the Prussian army was defeated at Jena, Napoleon entered the city determined to demoralise the vanquished and demonstrate the effectiveness of war. He removed the precious Quadriga and shipped it to Paris as part of the spoils. But the citizens rallied to the flag and Prussia's resistance inspired the entire German people to view her cause as their own. Ultimately they triumphed; Marshal Blücher returned the goddess to the Brandenburg Gate amid scenes of national rejoicing. Langhans' original intentions were quite forgotten in the din, even by the great architect Karl Frederick Schinkel, who sought to adorn the wreath of oak leaves decorating Viktoria's staff with the iron cross.

When German unification was finally achieved in 1871, not by democratic means but by 'blood and iron', the

Built as a gateway to peace in 1789, the Brandenburg Gate is Berlin's most enduring symbol

The goddess Viktoria's chariot and horses

celebrations centred on a triumphant procession through the Brandenburg Gate led by the Kaiser and his generals. Who would then have believed that, less than 50 years later, at the end of World War I, the Kaiser's grandson would be driving through the same arch for the last time into exile, bringing to an end more than 500 years of Hohenzollern rule?

In the crisis that followed, Germany was confronted by civil war, and revolutionary and government forces in turn took up machine-gun positions on top of the Gate. The darkest era in German history was dawning, when Nazi stormtroopers would process under torchlight through the Gate in celebration of a 1,000-year Reich that would be built on hatred, division and war. Instead came defeat and national humiliation: by 1945 Berlin lay in ruins and Soviet troops raised the red flag of Communism over the battered, pock-marked arch.

During the Cold War, the Gate became the symbol not of German unity but of her division. Western politicians eagerly seized photo-opportunities to eye the Gate ruefully across no-man's-land, while their Eastern counterparts did their best to obscure the view down Unter den Linden by hanging red banners across its columns. When the Wall finally came down in 1990, the Brandenburg Gate took on a new symbolic role – one of hope and renewal. It is a role more in keeping with Langhans' original vision of a gateway dedicated to peace.

Politics

In October 1990, Germany became one nation for the first time in more than 40 years and Berlin became its capital. The Christian Democratic Union (CDU) won the first all-city elections, but in view of Berlin's problems at that time – and in the spirit of compromise – it was decided to appoint a consensus government across party lines. The election of 1998 resulted in victory for the Social Democratic Party (SPD). Since then, however, a series of coalitions has complicated the political picture somewhat.

When conservative-leaning Chancellor Angela Merkel (raised and educated in easterly Brandenburg during GDR times) took office with a slim 1 per cent majority vote after November 2005's federal elections, she led a 'grand coalition' consisting of her own CDU party in partnership with the rival SPD plus the Christian Social Union (CSU).

The leftist-environmentalist Green Party (Alliance 90, *Die Grünen*) was part of the national coalition government between 1998 and October 2005.

Seat of government

Soon after 1991's elections, the municipal administration made a symbolic move from Rathaus Schöneberg, former home of the West Berlin council, to the city centre's Rotes Rathaus. In June 1991, the Bundestag voted to make Berlin the seat of Germany's government by 2000. The administration works in various parts of the city, but the Chamber itself convenes in the historic Reichstag.

In 1993, the Defence Ministry became one of the first to move back to Berlin. The choice of offices in the old Bendlerblock, where Admiral Tirpitz had masterminded the expansion of Germany's imperial navy before World War I, was seen by many as insensitive, but the minister, Volker Rühe, argued that the role it played in the von Stauffenberg plot against Hitler, in July 1944, gave it unimpeachable credentials.

Berlin's evolution

Mood swings have been rampant since Berlin regained *Hauptstadt* (capital city) status. Initial euphoria was evident during the heady days of 1989–90. Immediately afterwards, loss of its generous special-status Cold War subsidies caused a deep recession: unemployment rose in Germany to a record 5.2 million (10 per cent in the West, nearly 20 per cent in the East). By 2005, the jobless total had dipped to 4.5 million. Two years later, unemployment fell to a 14-year low at 3.6 million (8.7 per cent nationwide). With new industries and investments reviving the five ex-GDR eastern states, the general upswing continues. Unemployment has fallen to 3.4 million (7 per cent in the West, 14.7 per cent in the East, with the Berlin city-state gradually recovering at less than 14 per cent).

Economic hardships have lessened, as have crises of identity. The GDR, and the ideology it espoused, had been consigned to the scrapheap: socialism was declared moribund, the currency was pronounced worthless, and even such national symbols as the hammer-and-sickle flag were held up to ridicule. Frustration turned to resentment. West Berliners were perceived as spoiled, arrogant and lacking in ideals. Faced with an erosion in their own living standards, the 'Wessies' (West Berliners) blamed the 'Ossies' (East Berliners) for dragging the economy down. Looking for a scapegoat, elements on both sides found one in their respective immigrant communities – the Turks in the West, the 'guest workers' in the East. Resentment became so great that there were even those who, only half-jokingly, called for the rebuilding of the Wall, 'only this time five metres higher'. Now such statements are rarely heard; resilient Berliners have learned to live, recover and prosper together.

Germany is a parliamentary democracy. The head of the state is the Federal President, elected for five years by representatives of the Bundestag and the governments of the 16 *Länder* (states). There is a bicameral parliament comprising the *Bundestag* (House of Representatives) and the *Bundesrat* (Federal Council). There are six major parties: the Christian Democratic Union (CDU), the Christian Social Union (CSU), the Social Democratic Party (SPD), the Free Democratic Party (FDP), the Partei Deutscher Sozialisten (PDS) and the Greens.

The future

The issue of racism is particularly sensitive in Berlin, and in other parts of Germany. Clashes between right-wing factions and Turkish immigrants take place every now and again. Occasionally anti-Semitism creeps in and there have been a number of attacks on Jewish monuments and memorials.

A sense of perspective is needed when looking at Berlin's problems. The worries that preoccupy Berliners are much the same as those affecting the citizens of Europe as a whole. Looked at more objectively, despite all the problems that Berlin faces, the long-term future for the city looks bright. The levels of investment are unprecedented, as any visitor can see in the number and scale of building developments currently going on all over the city. Berlin has a level of subsidy which many cities can only dream of, a geographical position right at the heart of Europe, and exceptional opportunities for tourism. And no matter what Berliners have to say about one another, East and West, they have an equal capacity for hard work and a heartfelt desire to see their city succeed.

Ich bin ein Berliner

It is characteristic of Berliners that even in the most trying circumstances they retain their sense of humour. So it was to be expected that when President Kennedy came to the city in 1963 to show solidarity with the beleaguered inhabitants and proclaimed '*Ich bin ein Berliner*' ('I am a Berliner') there were more than a few wry smiles among his audience – a *Berliner* is also a kind of doughnut.

Berliners are, as they always have been, quick-witted, energetic, industrious, sentimental, generous, ebullient, sophisticated and arrogant. It is this last trait that is the origin of the term *Berliner Schnauze* or 'mouth', implying a tendency to shout people down, to feel superior, to be a bit of a 'know-all'. Two hundred years ago the poet Goethe put it rather more circumspectly: the Berliner, he suggested, was 'somewhat forward'. But the Berliners themselves talk of *Herz und Schnauze* ('heart and mouth') – they are, they will assure you (and it is difficult not to agree with them), big-hearted and thoroughly likeable.

Berlin, more than ever nowadays, is a cosmopolitan city. A significant proportion of the guest workers who began to arrive from Turkey, Yugoslavia and the Middle East in the

Classic Open Air concert, Gendarmenmarkt

Sculpture *Berlin* on Tauentzienstrasse, symbolising the four sectors into which the city was divided at the end of World War II

1960s and 1970s have set up home here, adding extra breadth and a little spice to the Berlin persona. There is the story of a visitor to a restaurant, who having asked the manager what it meant to be a Berliner was introduced to the staff – an Italian, a Lebanese, a Yugoslav and an Egyptian.

And what of the Ossies and Wessies, inhabitants of a long-divided Berlin now thrown together like a shy couple at a rowdy dance? Understanding between the two communities is not always easy, but the resilience, the courage and above all the humour typical of Berliners remains common to both. It was, after all, an East Berliner who apologised on behalf of Marx and Engels: 'Sorry, but it's not our fault. Maybe next time things will turn out better.'

Culture

'Its liberal, tolerant tradition, its contradictions, the sardonic humour of its people, and the sense of a living past that it has learned to integrate …'

Wim Wenders

film director, on the appeal of Berlin

Berlin takes its culture seriously, but no two Berliners can agree on what that culture is. The result is an almost anarchic diversity. Cultures, both mainstream and alternative, compete on every level but in an atmosphere of friendly rivalry.

To explore Berlin is to experience this range of cultures. Begin at the Ku'damm where you'll find the international culture that is available in every European city – Hollywood blockbusters, snackbars and clubs. Even cabaret, once notorious for its biting satire and subversive irony, has succumbed to the new internationalism.

For hard-hitting political satire or 1920s nostalgia, you'll have to look further, to the clubs around Friedrichstrasse, where nightlife was born at the turn of the 20th century. Culturally, Berlin has always embraced the notion of sexual liberation. Nollendorfplatz is still as much the focal point for the gay and lesbian community as it was many decades ago.

Berlin's high culture is more geographically dispersed. The city's peculiar status during the Cold War allowed it to play off the rival ideological camps to advantage. The result is at least two of everything (there are four opera houses and four major symphony orchestras).

Kreuzberg and Prenzlauer Berg are citadels of the alternative culture, spawning here-today, gone-tomorrow art galleries, events and happenings, exhibitions and impromptu performances. Kreuzberg is known as 'little Istanbul' because of its large Turkish community – the streets between Hallesches Tor and Schlesisches Tor have a distinct flavour of the Orient, with bazaars and exotic restaurants. Culture is not what it was in Berlin – and therein lies the secret of its success. For while other cities look back with nostalgia to their artistic and cultural heritage, Berliners look forward to the future, which is why the city is set to win a place in the cultural heart of Europe.

The old Arsenal (Zeughaus) now houses the German Historical Museum

Impressions

Berlin has been more generously endowed than any other city in Europe of its size with lakes, forests and rivers, as anyone flying over the metropolis on a clear day will immediately appreciate. No wonder that even Berliners used to the hectic pace of life here drop everything and 'head for the hills'. The natural beauty of the surroundings makes up for the disorderly character of the city itself, partly the legacy of wartime destruction, partly the result of the Berliner's obsession with rebuilding ever bigger and better.

Arriving

All three Berlin airports are surprisingly near the city centre. Most international flights from Western Europe and the USA currently pass through Tegel, which is about 8km (5 miles) to the northwest and can be reached by bus or taxi. However, Schönefeld has been gaining importance as the region's main international gateway; it is situated 20km (12 miles) southeast, directly accessible by S-Bahn and the DB German Rail's Airport Express service. Within the next few years, the airport will be greatly expanded and renamed Berlin Brandenburg International (code BBI), and is due to open in October 2011, replacing all of Berlin's airports. Historic 1920s Tempelhof (the world's oldest commercial airport and third-largest building complex), now used only by commuter flights and about 15 minutes from central Berlin (*U-Bahn to Platz der Luftbrücke*), is tentatively (and controversially) scheduled to close as of 2008.

Berlin has excellent rail links, although it is only since the Lehrter Bahnhof was transformed into the new Hauptbahnhof in 2006 (served by a new line tunnelling under the heart of Berlin) that there has finally been a central station for all long distance and regional services.

Getting your bearings

The Wall is a thing of the past, but Berlin is still in many respects two cities, divided by the great park called the Tiergarten. Berlin's most famous street, the Kurfürstendamm (known locally as the Ku'damm), is in the West. It is, first and foremost, a shopping street, although there are theatres, cinemas, restaurants and nightclubs here too. Many of Berlin's largest and best hotels are also in the Charlottenburg district.

The historic heart of Berlin is in the East, starting with the Brandenburg Gate, which presides over one end of Unter den Linden. This majestic avenue was once the main thoroughfare of

Imperial Berlin, and shops and cafés are beginning to appear again, although nightlife comes to a stop much earlier here than in the West. Former East Berlin contains most of the city's historic buildings and monuments, as well as Museumsinsel (Museum Island). Berlin's unsightly but unmistakable television tower, the Fernsehturm, is also in the East. More than 300m (984ft) high, it offers a panorama of the entire city. An alternative viewing point in the West is the Europa-Center.

Central Berlin was devastated by Allied bombing during World War II. As a consequence, Potsdamer Platz became a wasteland on border territory. Since unification in 1990, the area has been redeveloped as a new business, cultural and residential quarter which attracts Berliners and visitors alike. The International Film Festival is held here in February and the Potsdamer Platz arcades welcome shoppers. Cafés, restaurants, cinemas and a theatre for musicals, a casino and hotels crowd around the Marlene-Dietrich-Platz.

Souvenir stalls can be found near many of Berlin's popular sights, such as the Brandenburg Gate

Road system

Berlin is already fully integrated into the German road system. A ring road surrounds the city with access from north and south. There are major routes out of Berlin to Rostock and Hamburg in the north, Hannover and Braunschweig in the west, Nürnberg (Nuremberg) and München (Munich) in the south, and Frankfurt an der Oder and Szczecin (Poland) in the east.

Having arrived in Berlin, leave your car in a long-stay car park. The public transport system is efficient and not overly expensive, while driving can be a nightmare. Some road surfaces, especially in the East, remain uneven and poorly lit and there are trams to negotiate. The one-way system presents problems of its own, such as long stretches of road with no left turn.

Getting around

Berlin is a very large city, and the discouragingly long streets induce fatigue all too easily. The best advice is to restrict walking to a stroll through the Tiergarten or Grunewald Forest, which is more pleasurable. Also, when walking beware of straying on to cycle lanes (marked in red). It is quite accepted for cyclists to travel along these dedicated lanes at great speed and with little regard for wayward pedestrians.

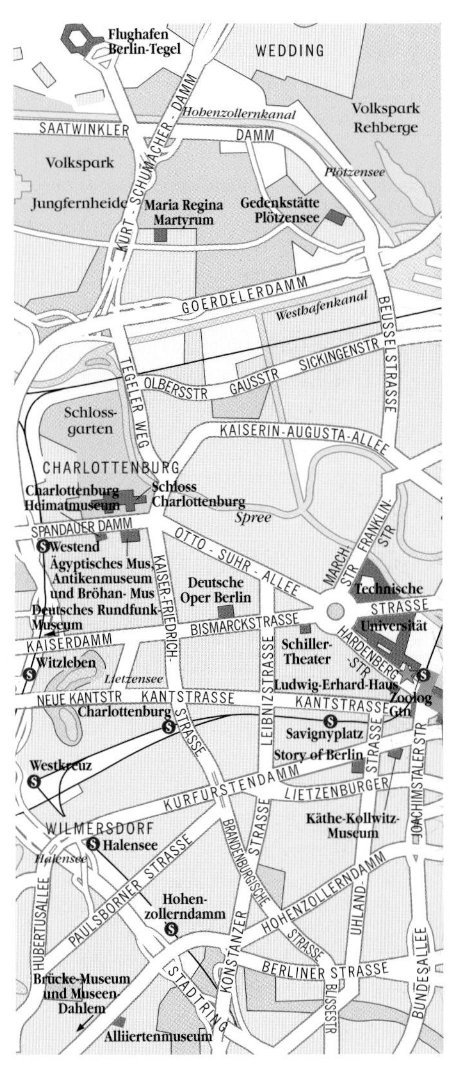

Berlin (see pp112–13 for orange route)

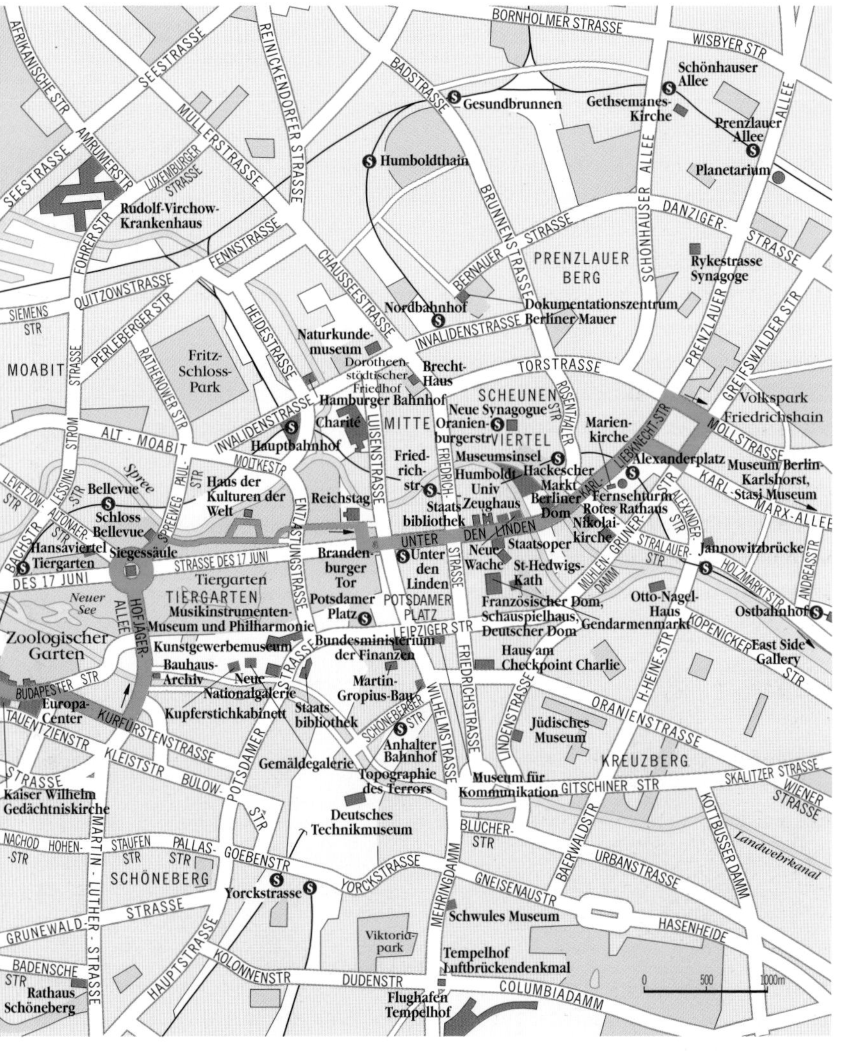

Maps and streets

An up-to-date map is a priority, and here the stress should be on up-to-date. As with other cities in the former Eastern Bloc there has been an orgy of name-changing: at the last count more than 80 streets were affected, as well as several U-Bahn and S-Bahn stations (Marx-Engels Platz, for example, has reverted to Hackescher Markt). Generally speaking, the process is complete, but there are likely to be some isolated changes in the future (there are plans to name a street after the former Chancellor and Mayor of West Berlin, Willy Brandt, for example – Wilhelmstrasse has been mentioned as a possibility). Bear in mind, too, that in some of the outlying suburbs the old street signs remain in place. That being said, the most reliable map is produced by the German automobile association – the Berlin ADAC Stadtplan. This includes plans of the Tiergarten and Mitte as well as the new postal codes, plus tourist information on the reverse.

Transport

Few cities in Europe have such a comprehensive public transport system as Berlin. Single journeys are relatively expensive, so before you do anything else buy a travel card from the BVG information counter at Hauptbahnhof on Europaplatz, or from the BVG-Pavillon on Hardenbergplatz opposite Bahnhof Zoo, where maps and timetables are also on sale. The 24-hour ticket (24-Stunden-Karte) and the weekly Umweltkarte allow unlimited travel on the entire BVG network (buses, trains, trams, and even the ferry

A train crosses the Oberbaumbrücke, linking districts that were once divided by the Wall

Pedestrians beware! Cyclists are to be found everywhere in Berlin

from Wannsee to Kladow). The weekly ticket allows an additional adult and up to three children (from 6–13 years) to travel free from Mondays to Fridays from 8pm to 3am and all day on Saturdays, Sundays and public holidays.

There are two complementary urban rail networks: the S-Bahn (Schnellbahn/rapid transit), which dates from 1882 and has long, elevated sections punctuated by some striking *Jugendstil* stations; and the U-Bahn (underground). Both systems are interchangeable, but the S-Bahn provides access to the more outlying suburbs such as Wannsee, Oranienburg and Köpenick.

The distinctive yellow double-decker buses round off the transportation network and are also extremely useful for getting about the central areas of the city and the western suburbs. The Ku'damm is made easily manageable by hopping on and off buses, and route 100, which leaves from Bahnhof Zoo, provides an excellent service linking the West End with Unter den Linden and Alexanderplatz. (Alight by the stairs at the back.) An excellent night-bus service operates throughout the city.

Cycling in central Berlin is feasible provided one knows where one is going. The best places to cycle, however, are the forests and lakes of the outlying suburbs, and these can be reached more easily by rail (cycles may be taken onto the S-Bahn – use the doors marked with the relevant symbol).

Language

Generally, language presents few difficulties in Berlin. Berliners do

Crowds turn out for the Berlin Marathon in late September every year

have a distinctive accent, but visitors with a knowledge of standard German will encounter few problems. English is in increasingly common use, especially in restaurants, but East Berliners are less likely to speak it as Russian was formerly the first foreign language taught in East German schools.

Manners and mores

Much is made of the differences between Berliners and other Germans, and certainly Berliners are more relaxed and easy-going than many of their compatriots. But Berliners are Germans nonetheless, and share the basic characteristics: respect for order and authority, a passion for cleanliness (though you might not think so wandering around Zoo station), and a certain formality. So say *guten Tag* before asking for something in a shop, and *auf Wiedersehen* when leaving. If you're trying to weave your way through a crowd say *entschuldigen Sie* or 'pardon' – which is also what to say if you tread on someone's toes. Jaywalking is frowned upon, so don't be surprised if you get lots of disapproving looks for doing so. The Germans also have a deserved reputation for obeying the lights at pedestrian crossings. Berliners are somewhat wayward in this respect, but again don't be surprised if someone in the crowd seizes your arm or gives you a short lecture on road safety. Berliners tend to dress informally when dining out, but in nightclubs the usual rules – smart but casual – apply.

When to visit

With its countless indoor attractions and places of interest, Berlin is a year-round destination. However, if you do come in winter bring plenty of warm clothing: the average temperature hovers around 0°C, and it can get much colder. Summers tend to be very changeable – not exceptionally hot and with plenty of rain. But when the sun shines, the forests of Grunewald and the lakes at Wannsee, Müggelsee and elsewhere fill up with hikers, swimmers and tennis enthusiasts or techno-fans. It is here, rather than in the city, that one can still sample the famous *Berliner Luft* or fresh air.

Perhaps the best time to visit is the spring and early autumn when sightseeing is less tiring but visiting out-of-town venues is still a practical option. Cinema buffs will want to come in February for the Berlin Film Festival; jazz enthusiasts in July; joggers should visit in mid-autumn, when the marathon takes place.

Getting around Berlin is not a problem

Berlin

'It is not at all easy to visit or live in a city that is always on the move, always in the process of becoming something else and never content to stay as it is.'

FRANZ HESSEL
writer

Alexanderplatz

'Alex', as the square is affectionately known to Berliners, has had, and undoubtedly will see, better days. It was originally a wool and cattle market and takes its name from Tsar Alexander I of Russia, who once reviewed the troops here. During the 19th century Alexanderplatz became the centre of working-class Berlin and a focal point of social unrest. The criminal underworld was drawn to the square like a magnet – Franz Biberkopf, the hero of Alfred Döblin's 1929 novel *Berlin Alexanderplatz,* is a convicted murderer who, after his release from prison, sells newspapers on the square.

A section of the wall at the Museum of the Allies

After World War II, Alexanderplatz became a showcase for the 'new' Communist architecture but the end product is predictably sterile: a vast windswept space, intermittently scattered with *imbiss* (snack) stands and market stalls and dominated by the Park Inn Hotel, whose single virtue is the restaurant and casino on the 37th floor with panoramic views. Perhaps Alex's greatest moment was on 4 November 1989, when half a million East Berliners gathered to protest against the old regime (which collapsed a mere five days later). Sightseeing attractions are thin on the ground; the most noteworthy is Erich John's **Weltzeituhr** (World Time Clock) in the southern part of the square.

The regeneration of what Berliners refer to as 'the Alex' is well under way, with the opening of one of the city's largest new shopping malls, ALEXA, in

September 2007. **Galeria Kaufhof**, a department store anchoring part of the vast square since the 1970s, has been extensively refurbished and a glass-panelled, six-storey retail development called **Die Mitte-Shopping am Alexanderplatz** is on schedule for completion by the end of 2008.
U-Bahn or S-Bahn to Alexanderplatz.

Alliiertenmuseum (Museum of the Allies)

Documenting the presence of the Allied forces in Berlin, which lasted until 1994, the collection concentrates on the period of the Blockade and the 1948 *Luftbrücke* (airlift). You can find memorabilia such as tanks and even music, and there are temporary exhibitions every year. Don't miss the old stop-and-search border checkpoint outside where the sign 'You are now leaving the American Sector' once stood.
Zehlendorf, Clayallee 135. Tel: (030) 818 1990. www.alliiertenmuseum.de.
Open: daily 10am–6pm. Free admission.
U-Bahn to Oskar-Helene-Heim.

Alexanderplatz, with the World Time Clock

The Bauhaus

The Bauhaus was founded in Weimar by Walter Gropius, in the climate of frenetic renewal after World War I. Breaking down the artificial divisions between art and architecture, Gropius and his collaborators sought to create a unity of design and an art that was functional rather than decorative, serving the needs of ordinary people. Technology was pressed into service, as well as modern materials like concrete, glass and tubular steel. Awareness of the possibilities of mass production ensured that the Bauhaus's influence would reach far beyond the boundaries of Germany.

The Bauhaus was a school of experiment with an unusually free and challenging curriculum. Its teachers were outstanding artistic figures in their own right, some with international reputations: Paul Klee, Vassily Kandinsky, Oskar Schlemmer and László Moholy-Nagy. There were workshops in furniture, metalwork, print and advertising, photography,

The entrance to the workshop at Dessau

The Bauhaus complex at Dessau

wall painting, ceramics, weaving and stage design, loosely coordinated by a directorate of Gropius, Hannes Mayer and Mies van der Rohe.

From the outset, the Bauhaus suffered from financial and political constraints. Forced out of Weimar by local right-wing politicians, the school moved to Dessau in 1925 and subsequently to Berlin, where persistent Nazi harassment finally forced it to close in 1933. Some of the more prominent artists like Gropius and Schlemmer escaped to the USA, where their aims and achievements were already well known and from where they continued to exert a major influence. Others, less fortunate, ended their days in concentration camps.

Bauhaus-Archiv

This is a fascinating museum of design relating to the history of the Bauhaus (1919–33), one of the most influential artistic movements of the 20th century. The sleek white building with gentle curves in which the exhibition is housed was designed by Walter Gropius in 1964. On display is a representative selection of architectural models and plans, paintings, furniture and domestic objects.

Look out for paintings by Klee and Kandinsky, theatre designs by Schlemmer, a silver tea and coffee set by Marianne Brandt (1924), Marcel Breuer's metal-framed chair (1928), and Moholy-Nagy's experimental 'light-space modulator' (1922–30), an extraordinary amalgam of wood, metal, glass and plexiglass which rotates when operated by a button. The overall impression is of having seen many of the items somewhere before, and indeed one has – in the design of countless everyday objects which can be found in today's homes.

Tiergarten, Klingelhöferstrasse 14. Tel: (030) 254 0020. www.bauhaus.de. Open: Wed–Mon 10am–5pm. Closed: Tue. Admission charge. Buses: 106, 129, 219 & 231 to Lützowplatz.

Berliner Dom (Berlin Cathedral)

Dominating the lower end of Unter den Linden, Berlin's Protestant cathedral was intended as a monument to the Hohenzollern dynasty, more than 90 of whose members lie in the vaults below. A pet project of Kaiser William II's, it was designed by Carl Julius Raschdorff in High Renaissance style and opened in 1905 on the site of an earlier cathedral. During World War II it suffered major bomb damage, and needed extensive restoration. The dome, which bears more than a passing resemblance to St Peter's in Rome, gives the interior a light and airy feel, in stark contrast to the blackened and rather forbidding exterior. There is an exhibition of historical photographs in the cathedral, which is also the venue for occasional organ recitals.

Museumsinsel/Am Lustgarten. Tel: (030) 2026 9136. www.berlinerdom.de. Open: Mon–Sat 9am–8pm, Sun 11.30am–8pm. Guided tours in English, Thur 3–5.30pm, Sat 10.30am–1.30pm. Admission charge. S-Bahn to Hackescher Markt. Buses: 100, 157 & 348.

Blockhaus Nikolskoe

In 1819 Frederick William III built this wooden cabin in a secluded pine forest as a romantic retreat for his daughter Charlotte and her prospective husband, the future Tsar Nicholas I of Russia (Nikolskoe is Russian for 'belonging to Nicholas'). Perhaps this act of consideration helped cement the marriage, which, by all accounts, was a happy one. Today, the Blockhaus is a popular restaurant (crowded in season) with superb views over the Havel.

Berlin Cathedral on Unter den Linden

Once you've feasted your eyes, follow the slope to the **Church of Saints Peter and Paul**, which is modelled on a Russian original. It was built in 1834 by Friedrich Wilhelm Stüler and has a distinctive onion dome.
Wannsee, Nikolskoer Weg 15. Tel: (030) 805 2914. Restaurant open: Fri–Wed, summer 9am–10pm; winter 10am–8pm. Bus: A16 from Wannsee.

Botanischer Garten (Botanical Garden)

A stroll through the Botanical Garden is the perfect way to relax after visiting the Dahlem museums (*see pp42–3, 46*). Berlin's first botanical gardens were laid out in the grounds of the royal palace in the 18th century. The move to Dahlem took place in 1899 and the gardens are now home to one of the world's largest botanical collections, with over 18,000 types of plants and flowers. Set in the beautifully landscaped grounds and beech woods are the *Jugendstil* (Art Nouveau) glasshouses, housing orchids, palms, ferns, cacti and other exotica against a background of lily ponds and waterfalls. Unless you are a dedicated botanist, give the adjoining museum a miss and stop off instead at the café near the Unter den Eichen exit.
Steglitz, Königin Luise-Strasse 6–8. Tel: (030) 838 501. Open: daily 9am–4pm. Guided tours in English, but an application is required two weeks in advance. Admission charge. U-Bahn to Rathaus Steglitz & S-Bahn to Botanischer Garten. Buses: 101, 148 & 180.

Berlin environs

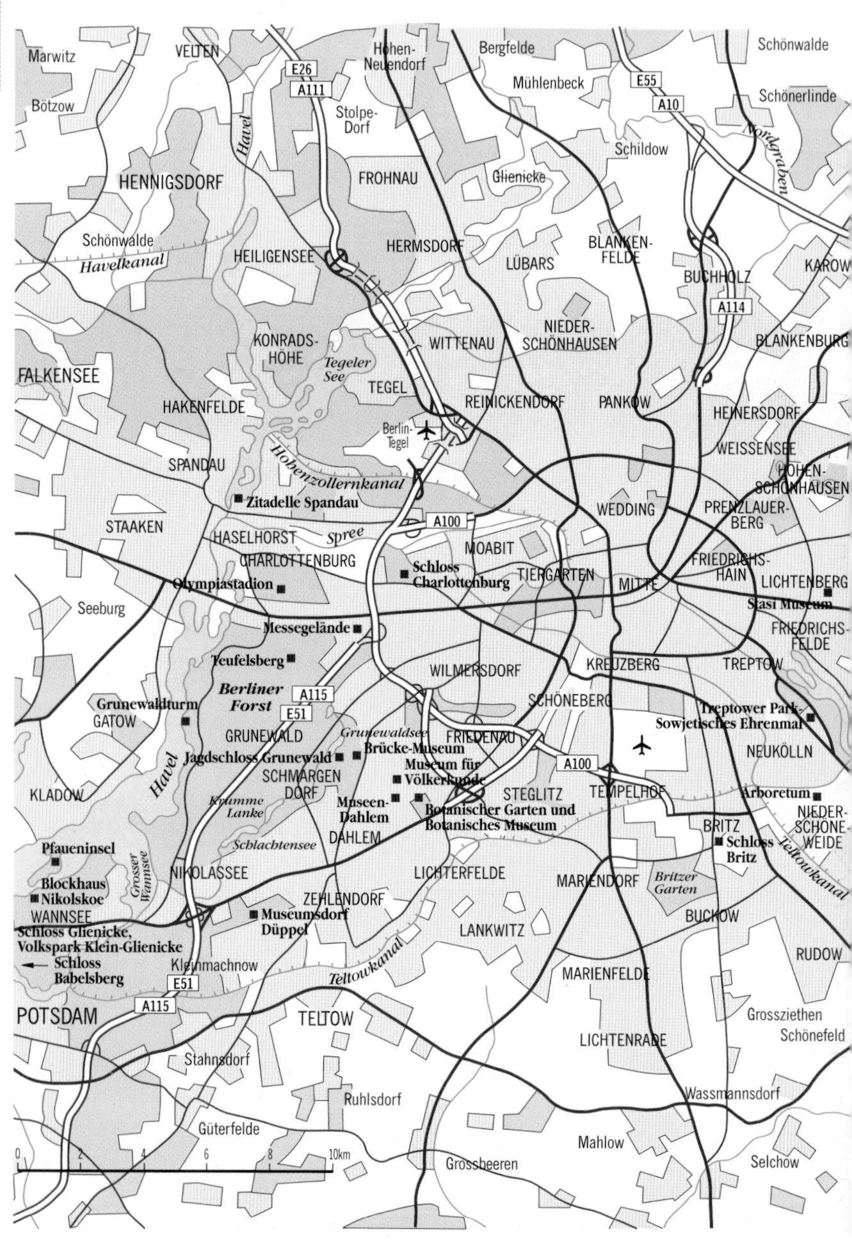

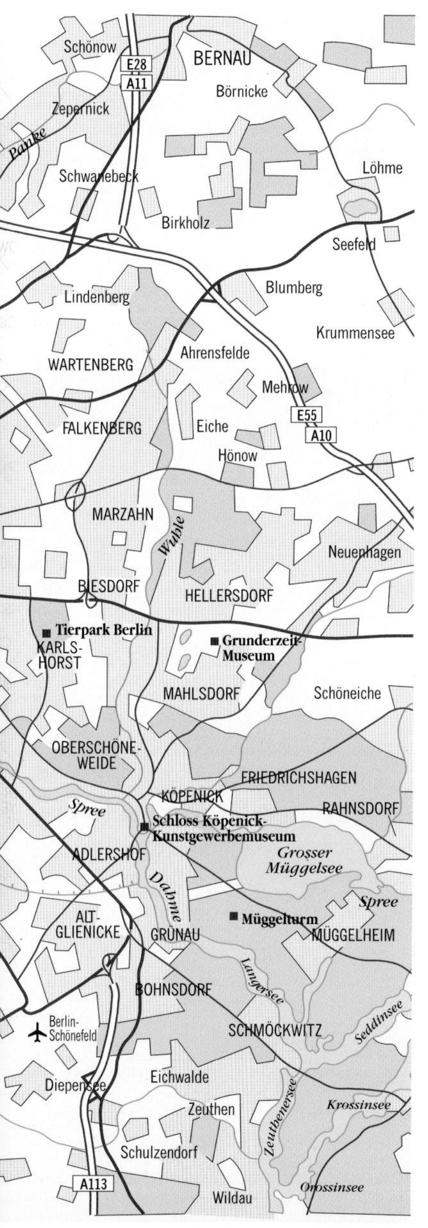

Brandenburger Tor (Brandenburg Gate)

Built on the site of a toll-gate which once marked the western end of the city, the present gate has been modelled on the Propylaeum, which is the entrance to the Acropolis in Athens, and was built between 1788 and 1791 to a design by Carl Gotthard Langhans. The Quadriga surmounting it was added three years later by the architect Johann Gottfried Schadow (*see pp10–11*).

Mitte. U-Bahn to Unter den Linden. Bus: 100.

Brecht-Haus

This house-museum is where the German playwright Bertolt Brecht (1898–1956) spent the last three years of his life with his actress wife Helene Weigel. First impressions are of austere simplicity and a no-nonsense attitude to a life which revolved wholly around work.

The guided tour begins in the small study, an unpretentious room lined with bookshelves stacked to the ceiling with volumes testifying to the erudition and eclectic tastes of the man. Standard German classics such as Kleist, Schiller, Lessing and Thomas Mann rub shoulders with Virgil, Shakespeare, Sophocles, Chinese and Japanese texts, revolutionary tomes by Lenin and Karl Marx, detective novels and collections of American protest songs. Noh masks and a scroll painting of Confucius are further evidence of Brecht's interest in oriental cultures.

The Brecht-Haus museum on Chausseestrasse

BERTOLT BRECHT

Brecht achieved overnight fame in 1928 with the Berlin production of *Die Dreigroschenoper* (*The Threepenny Opera*). Kurt Weill wrote the music and his wife, Lotte Lenya, starred as Pirate Jenny. The show was a commercial and literary success but the serious political commitment underlying Brecht's work forced him to leave Nazi Germany in 1933 for the USA. It was during this exile that he wrote his most influential plays, including *Mother Courage and her Children* and *The Caucasian Chalk Circle.* In 1948, the East German authorities invited him back to Berlin, where he established his own theatre company, the Berliner Ensemble, still in existence today.

The furnishings are utilitarian, the décor sparse, the floor bare. Brecht, a committed revolutionary, once told a friend: 'It's a really commendable idea to live in houses with furniture that is at least 120 years old; an early capitalist environment until there is a socialist one.'

The large study, with its view over the garden, was Brecht's favourite working place, with each table assigned to a separate project. Missing from this sanitised museum setting is the sense of creative discovery and the pungent odour of cigar smoke. Late at night Brecht would retire upstairs to his bedroom and read the newspapers, while downstairs, Helene Weigel created her own, more homely, space. There is a lighter feel here, especially in the conservatory, with its potted plants, Meissen porcelain and domestic bric-a-brac. Both Brecht and Weigel are buried in the adjoining Dorotheenstädtischer Cemetery.

Mitte, Chausseestrasse 125.
Tel: (030) 283 0570. Open: Tue–Fri 10–11.30am, Thur also 5–6.30pm (except holidays), Sat 9.30am–12.30pm, Sun 11am–6pm. Closed: Mon. Guided tours only. Admission charge. U-Bahn to Zinnowitzer Strasse or Oranienburger Tor.

Icon of Berlin, the Brandenburg Gate

Bridges

There are more than 15 bridges spanning the Spree in central Berlin alone, yet, like the river itself, they are often overlooked. Here are just a handful of the more interesting ones.

Gertraudenbrücke

This bridge crosses Fischerinsel close to the point where Berlin and its twin settlement of Cölln were founded. It was built by the Great Elector Frederick William and is named after Gertraud, the patron saint of the poor and of travellers. It is a favourite with fishermen, who began plying their trade along this stretch of the river in the 13th century. Note the bronze water rats decorating the base of Gertraud's statue.

Jungfernbrücke

A little further north of the Gertraudenbrücke, the Jungfernbrücke is the last of what were once nine drawbridges spanning the river. It dates from 1798 and the drawbridge, still intact, rests on a pair of sturdy stone arches. Huguenot girls once sold their silk and lace wares here.

Lessingbrücke

This elegant iron bridge crosses the bend of the Spree north of the Tiergarten. It is named after one of Germany's best-known dramatists, Gotthold Ephraim Lessing (1729–81), and the four piers of red sandstone which complete the design are decorated with a number of scenes taken from his plays.

Moabiter Brücke

The next bridge along from the Lessingbrücke, on Bellevue Ufer, the Moabiter Brücke was built in 1894 and blends in well with the industrial warehouses. Its most prominent features are the streetlamps which serve to decorate the parapet, and the four bears (the bear being the symbol of Berlin).

Moltke Brücke

One of the most impressive of Berlin's bridges, the Moltke Brücke stands on Kronprinzen-Ufer, between the Kongresshalle and the Reichstag. It is named after Field Marshal Count Helmuth von Moltke, hero of the three wars which brought about German unification – against Denmark in 1864, Austria in 1866, and France in 1870. Predictably, the mood of the bridge is triumphant – splendidly bellicose Prussian eagles stand guard over the trophies of war, while martially clad cherubs sporting swords, as well as drums and trumpets, decorate the base of the iron lamp-posts. Completed in 1891, the bridge was destroyed during World War II and re-erected in 1986.

Monbijou Brücke

The name of this bridge, Monbijou, commemorates a royal palace, designed by Knobelsdorff as a residence for Frederick William I's widow in 1740. The palace occupied the site of the nearby park but was destroyed in 1945 and never rebuilt. The plain stone bridge is otherwise unremarkable, except that it offers fine views of the Bode-Museum (*see pp75–6*), arguably the most handsome of the buildings on Museum Island.

Schlossbrücke

Far and away Berlin's best-known bridge, and justifiably so, the Schlossbrücke (Palace Bridge) was designed by Karl Friedrich Schinkel in 1819 to replace the decaying Hundebrücke (Dog's Bridge). It stood between the former Schloss and the Lustgarten and still offers a commanding view of Schlüter's masterpiece, the Zeughaus, as well as the unmistakable Berliner Dom. The outstanding feature of the bridge, an admirable blend of iron and stone and a splendid engineering achievement, is the marble statues of Greek gods, executed a little later by pupils of Rauch, but to designs by Schinkel. These figures induced 19th-century Berliners, demonstrating a typically mischievous show of humour, to rechristen the bridge the Dolls' Bridge (Puppenbrücke). Less humorously, the Communists renamed the bridge in honour of Marx and Engels, but it has now reverted to its original name.

The views from the Schlossbrücke (Palace Bridge) are impressive

Brücke-Museum

An unlikely but delightful location for a museum, beside a lake on the fringes of the Grunewald forest. This is an essential port of call for anyone wishing to understand the development of modern art in the 20th century. Die Brücke (the bridge) was a group formed in Dresden in 1905 by Ludwig Kirchner, Fritz Bleyl, Erich Heckel and Karl Schmidt-Rottluff, self-taught artists with a keen interest in experiment. The result was the first wave of German Expressionism, a movement devoted to exploring man's inner landscape rather than objective reality, and characterised by bold use of colour and seemingly uncontrolled brush strokes. Die Brücke, which later included Emil Nolde, Max Pechstein and Otto Mueller, was clearly influenced by Gauguin, Van Gogh and, most importantly, Cézanne, who also had a major impact on the Cubists. The group moved to Berlin for commercial reasons in 1911 and flirted briefly with the artistic ideas of the New Secession; it broke up in 1913.

The museum owes its existence to the longest-surviving member of the group, Schmidt-Rottluff, who donated 74 of his own paintings on his 80th birthday in 1964. By the time the building was completed in 1967 considerable progress had been made in locating and purchasing the works of other artists,

The entrance to the Brücke-Museum

HEINRICH ZILLE (1858–1929)

A prolific artist and popular illustrator, Zille both amused and educated successive generations of Berliners with his witty, sometimes sentimental, but always provocative depictions of the daily lives of workers, the *demi-monde* and the criminal classes – to such an extent that over time it became known as Zille's *Milljöh* (milieu).

For many years, Zille was a regular contributor to satirical journals like *Die lustigen Blätter* and *Simplizissimus.*

There is a statue of Zille outside the Märkisches Museum, but his favourite habitat was the old pub, Zum Nussbaum, in the Nikolai Quarter.

Heinrich-Zille-Museum, *Mitte/Nikolaiviertel, Propststrasse 11* (see map, p105). *Tel: (030) 246 32502. www.heinrich-zille-museum.de. Open: daily 10am–8pm. Admission charge. U-Bahn or S-Bahn to Alexanderplatz.*

such as Heinrich Zille (*see panel, above*), from private collectors, a task made all the more valuable by the fact that many of the paintings had been destroyed in the Nazi era.

The museum is small – just three exhibition rooms – and conducive to quiet reflection. There is one drawback, though: only one of the artists is generally exhibited at any one time. Paintings to look out for include Kirchner's *Berlin Street Scene* (1913), Erich Heckel's *Young Man with Girl* (1905), Max Pechstein's *Fishing Boat* (1913) and Schmidt-Rottluff's portrait of Rosa Schapire (1911).

Zehlendorf, Bussardsteig 9. Tel: (030) 831 2029. www.bruecke-museum.de. Open: Wed–Mon 11am–5pm. Admission charge. Bus: 115 to Pücklerstrasse.

Bundesministerium der Finanzen (Federal Finance Ministry)

A mammoth edifice that is jam-packed with 20th-century history. Officially known as the Detlev-Rohwedder-Haus, designed by architect Ernst Sagebiel, constructed in 1934–6 as the Prussian War Ministry, the grey limestone complex soon morphed into Hermann Göring's Luftwaffe Air Ministry. When a succession of various post-war DDR bureaucracies took over, the building became 'ground zero' during the people's uprising on 17 June 1953.

Mitte, Wilhelmstrasse 97, corner of Leipzigerstrasse. U-Bahn to Mohrenstrasse.

Charlottenburg

This district was once a rural backwater but transformed at the turn of the last century into a thriving commercial and residential area with a population that increased from 30,000 to 300,000 in the space of three decades. All the following museums are either close to or part of Schloss Charlottenburg (*see pp41–2*).

Ägyptisches Museum (Egyptian Museum)

There are plans to reunite this collection with its other half, separated during World War II and currently housed in the Bode-Museum. Until then, the Charlottenburg branch offers the choice exhibits. Carl Richard Lepsius spent eight years in Egypt in the 1840s before returning with the biggest haul of Egyptian antiquities the world had ever seen. The Charlottenburg display is a joy from start to finish – beautifully presented and of superb quality.

The star exhibit in the main hall is the exquisite head of Queen Nefertiti, aunt of Tutankhamen. It was discovered in 1912 by the Berlin archaeologist Ludwig Borchardt among the plaster casts of an ancient sculpture workshop dating back to around 1340 BC. The stunningly beautiful queen wears a tall blue crown wound with a band of gold and semi-precious stones. The sacred serpent or Uraeus, symbol of royalty, is coiled above the forehead. The surviving eye is made from a shell of rock crystal, into which a black-paste iris is set.

Nefertiti's beauty may be unrivalled, but it is Queen Hatshepsut who has the distinction of being the only woman ever to rule Egypt as Pharaoh. The mottled granite bust of this unique ruler represents her as an honorary man, complete with ceremonial beard. Another striking exhibit is the so-called Berlin Green Head, dating from the Ptolemaic period (about 300 BC). The forceful intelligence of the subject, a priest, is superbly captured by the sculptor. Elsewhere in the museum are bronzes, sarcophagi, papyri, jewellery, mummies, death masks, vials of perfume, vases, gaming boards and musical instruments dating from 5000 BC to AD 300.

In the entrance to the former livery stables stands the 2,000-year-old Kalabasha Gate. Constructed under the Ptolemies, it was later decorated with reliefs of the Emperor Augustus, posing rather improbably as Pharaoh.
Schlossstrasse 70. Tel: (030) 266 3660. www.smb.spk-berlin.de. Open: Tue–Sun 10am–6pm. Admission charge. U-Bahn to Richard-Wagner-Platz. Buses: 109, 110 & 145.

Bröhan-Museum

Based on the private collection of Professor Karl Bröhan, who presented it to the people of Berlin in 1983, this unusual museum consists of Art Nouveau, *Jugendstil* and Art Deco furniture, glass, ceramics, silver and industrial design from the turn of the 20th century to the 1930s.

New techniques of burnishing and glazing, developed in the 1870s, revolutionised ceramics and glass design throughout Europe and the USA. In Berlin, a leading role was played by the chemical research institute attached to the Royal Porcelain Manufacturers (KPM) under Hermann Seger, examples of whose work can be seen in room 18.

Equally striking are the metal-mounted pieces of Bohemian glass in the Salon Hector Guimard, one of a number of rooms named after a leading manufacturer or designer. There are some fine early 20th-century

paintings and drawings, too, notably works by Willy Jaeckel, Karl Hagemeister, Hans Balushchek and Jean Lambert-Rucki.
Schlossstrasse 1a. Tel: (030) 326 9600. www.broehan-museum.de. Open: Tue–Sun 10am–6pm (Thur 10am–8pm). Admission charge. Buses: 109, 145 & 210.

Charlottenburg Heimatmuseum (Charlottenburg Homeland History Museum)
Maps, photographs and models trace the history and development of this famous Berlin district.
Schlossstrasse 69. Tel: (030) 343 03201. Open: Tue–Fri 10am–5pm, Sun 11am–5pm. Free admission. Buses: 109, 110 & 145.

Museum für Vor- und Frühgeschichte (Museum of Pre- and Early History)
This museum began life as a haphazard collection of curios assembled by the Hohenzollerns. The tribal history of the Germanic peoples is illustrated with a fascinating array of artefacts, including Bronze Age weapons and necklaces originating in the Carpathian mountains. Sadly, there are only copies of what was once the prize exhibit, Heinrich Schliemann's fabulous Trojan treasure discovered in 1873 and wrongly attributed to King Priam himself. In 1945, the hoard was looted by Soviet troops and spirited away to Moscow. There are plans to loan out the exhibits, but the thorny problem of ownership has yet to be resolved.
In the West Wing of the Schloss. Tel: (030) 326 74811. Open: Tue–Fri 10am–6pm, Sat–Sun 11am–6pm. Admission charge. Buses: 109, 145, 210 & X21.

Schloss Charlottenburg
This exquisite palace, belonging to the Prussian royal house of Hohenzollern, has been miraculously recreated from the original plans after being almost totally destroyed during World War II.

Charlottenburg was a bucolic Eden in 1695 when the cultivated Electoress Sophie Charlotte, a noted patron of artists and philosophers, commissioned Johann Arnold Nering to design her a modest rural retreat between Berlin and Potsdam. The enhanced status of the Hohenzollerns after 1701, when the Elector became King Frederick I of Prussia, was reflected in the enlargement of house and grounds under the supervision of Johann Eosander von Göthe. The transformation of the palace into a miniature Versailles was the brainchild of Frederick the Great, who instructed the inspired architect Georg Wenzeslaus von Knobelsdorff to build a new wing in rococo style, including a suite of royal apartments. Carl Gotthard Langhans designed the theatre at the west end of the Orangery and the tea house in the grounds, the Belvedere (1788). Finally, in 1810, Frederick William III honoured the memory of his wife by commissioning a mausoleum from Karl Friedrich Schinkel (*see pp44–5*).

The encroachment of the city has unfortunately foreshortened the approach to the palace, but it is still impressive. An equestrian statue by Andreas Schlüter, representing the Great Elector in characteristically martial mood, dominates the courtyard. It originally stood on the Lange Brücke outside the Berlin Schloss.

Visitors are taken on a guided tour of the ground-floor apartments of the Old Wing, lasting approximately one hour. The tasteful elegance of the Gobelin rooms with their magnificent tapestries, delicately painted harpsichords and French paintings, the red-braid room, a dazzling spectacle of damask and gilded stucco, and the porcelain chamber with its magnificent painted ceiling, all serve as a reminder that there was more to the Prussian monarchy than blustering ambition and military aggrandisement.

The highlights of the New Wing, on the eastern side of the palace, are the breathtaking Golden Gallery, a rococo masterpiece, and the sumptuous White Hall, both designed for Frederick the Great. It is easy to imagine Frederick playing the flute in these refined surroundings, accompanied on the harpsichord by the most talented of Bach's sons, Carl Philip Emmanuel. Queen Luise's bedroom, designed by Schinkel, is also on the first floor and there are paintings of the French 18th-century school, including Watteau's *Departure for Cythera* and works by Boucher and Pesne.

On the western side of the building is the Great Orangery, now used for exhibitions, and the sedate Langhans Building, a museum of pre- and early history. Directly behind it, an avenue of fir trees leads to the Mausoleum. This is the burial place of a number of Prussian rulers and their subjects, including Kaiser William I and Queen Luise, whose tomb, by Christian Daniel Rauch, is in impeccable taste.

The landscaped English Garden unrolls park-like into the distance. Far to the right, on the banks of the Spree, is the compact Belvedere, designed by Langhans. It is now a museum of the history of Berlin porcelain, with high-quality pieces from the factories of Wegely, Gotzkowsky and the Royal Porcelain Manufacturers (KPM). The formal French Garden, with its sculpted lawns, shrubs, lakes and fountains, begins behind the green cupola of the palace.

Charlottenburg, Luisenplatz.
Tel: (331) 969 4202. Open: Tue–Sun 10am–5pm. Admission charge.
U-Bahn to Richard-Wagner-Platz.
Buses: 109, 110, 121, 145 & 309.

Dahlem museums

All the following museums are located in the scenic suburb of Dahlem in a purpose-built complex of buildings, completed in the 1960s. Only one ticket is required for all the collections.

Schloss Charlottenburg, one of Berlin's architectural gems

Ethnologisches Museum (Ethnography Museum)

The Museum of Ethnography was founded in 1873, although its earliest holdings can be traced back to the private collection of the Great Elector in the 17th century. The variety of artefacts from all around the world is so rich and absorbing that it is possible to spend hours here. If time is pressing, try at least not to miss the collection of Oceanian boats, completely reassembled and rigged out as they were in the 18th century. They include a *tongiaki* (a kind of catamaran from the island of Tonga) and an ocean-going sailing vessel from the island of Santa Cruz – a marvellous example of the technology of boat-building. There is also a beautifully decorated male clubhouse from the Palau Islands in the Western Pacific.

The museum is divided into eight regional departments. Ancient America includes fine examples of Pre-Columbian gold craftsmanship, Aztec stone figures and the largest collection of Peruvian pottery in Europe. From Africa there are Benin bronzes, carved figures of gods from Cameroon and terracottas from Ife (Nigeria). The Asian display has, among other things, Tang ceramics and, best of all, Indonesian shadow-puppets, masks and theatre puppets. Headphones near the museum entrance bring you music from around the world played on authentic instruments.

Schinkel's vision

He was Germany's greatest architect, but he was much more than that: Karl Friedrich Schinkel (1781–1841) was a sculptor, a painter, a set designer, an interior decorator, a towering intellect and a visionary. His legacy to Berlin is cast in stone – his monument, the city itself and particularly its finest avenue, Unter den Linden. (*Also see Schinkel*

Schauspielhaus (National Theatre)

Museum, p51.) Schinkel was born in Neuruppin in the Mark Brandenburg, the son of a Protestant pastor. His interest in architecture was fostered by the precocious Friedrich Gilly under whose father he began his training at the Bauakademie (Building Academy) in Berlin. The regulation Grand Tour of Europe followed, firing his imagination, but ultimately leading to frustration – the political turbulence of the Napoleonic period was hardly the climate for ambitious building schemes. Ever the Renaissance man, Schinkel turned instead to painting in a thoroughly Romantic style, inspired partly by the medieval Gothic architecture he had seen on his travels.

A fervent patriot, he volunteered for the Prussian militia and later designed the nation's most revered award, the Iron Cross. In 1816, Schinkel received his first major Berlin commission, the Neue Wache (Guardhouse). From this time on, he had to tame his Romantic inclinations in the face of the Hohenzollern royal house's preference for the Classical style: undaunted, Schinkel produced a masterpiece. The Schauspielhaus (National Theatre), situated on Gendarmenmarkt, followed. The theatre opened in 1821 with a play by Goethe and scenery by Schinkel himself, but it was typical of this shy man that when he was called to acknowledge the applause of the audience, he had already sneaked off home.

Nikolaikirche

A flurry of commissions followed: the Altes Museum, the Nikolaikirche in Potsdam, the Friedrichswerdersche Kirche and Schloss Babelsberg. In everything he undertook, Schinkel was conscientious to a fault – no detail was too small for his attention, even a door knob or a lampholder. But there was a price to pay for all this industry. By the end of the 1830s, Schinkel, one of the world's greatest workaholics, was thoroughly exhausted. He collapsed with a stroke in October 1841 and died.

Dahlem Museum cluster

Museum für Indische Kunst (Museum of Indian Art)

This museum neatly captures the richness and diversity of the culture of India. Artefacts range from prehistoric terracotta and stone sculptures to miniature paintings and exquisite examples of craftsmanship in metal, ivory and jade. The art of the Buddhist cave monasteries which once lined the famous Silk Road is also represented.

Museum für Ostasiatische Kunst (Museum of Far Eastern Art)

One of the best collections in Europe of prints and paintings from China, Japan and Korea, including some superb colour woodblock prints from Japan's Edo period (late 18th century). Other exhibits include a ceremonial axe from China (12th century BC) and finely carved lacquerware boxes.

GENERAL INFORMATION

Lansstrasse 8. Berlin-Dahlem.
Tel: (030) 930 1438. www.smb.museum.
Open: Tue–Fri 10am–6pm, Sat–Sun 11am–6pm. U-Bahn to Dahlem Dorf.
Buses: 110, 183, X11 & X83.

DDR Museum (GDR Museum)

In a Spree riverside building across from the Berliner Dom (*see map, p21*), this museum provides an in-depth look at the typical residence of an East Berlin family during the socialist decades. Mundane living-room furnishings and bathroom appliances are genuine period artefacts, as is the 'Trabi' car parked alongside. The TV stays tuned to documentaries recalling the years behind the Wall.
Mitte, Karl-Liebknecht-Strasse 1.
Tel: (030) 847 1273. Open: Tue–Fri 9am–8pm (Thur 10am–10pm), Sat–Sun

11am–6pm. Admission charge. U-Bahn to Alexanderplatz or S-Bahn to Hackescher Markt.

Denkmal für die ermordeten Juden Europas (Memorial to the Murdered Jews of Europe)

Inaugurated in 2005, Peter Eisenman's stark concept, on sloping 2ha (5-acre) terrain directly south of the Brandenburg Gate (and symbolically near the site of Adolf Hitler's chancellery and bunker), comprises 2,711 concrete slabs set in a wavelike pattern amidst narrow pathways. *Tiergarten, Cora-Berliner Strasse 1. Tel: (030) 740 72929. Open: daily 10am–8pm. Admission charge for the below-ground Information and Documentation Centre. U-Bahn to Französische Strasse & S-Bahn to Potsdamer Platz.*

Deutscher Dom (German Cathedral)

The German Cathedral is situated on the southern side of the Gendarmenmarkt and nicely complements its French twin, the Französischer Dom (French Cathedral) opposite (*see pp50–51*). The architect of the elongated domed tower, Karl von

The Dahlem museum complex was specifically designed to house exhibitions

The Memorial to the Murdered Jews of Europe

Gontard, was described by Frederick the Great as an 'ass' – and this was before the cupola collapsed in 1781. Another architect, Georg Christian Unger, was called in to rectify matters. The building is used for exhibitions.
Mitte, Gendarmenmarkt.
Tel: (030) 227 3043. Free admission.
U-Bahn to Französische Strasse.

Deutsches Historisches Museum

Originally imperial Berlin's 17th-century Schinkel-designed armoury (Zeughaus), reopened in 2005 after renovation and expansion by contemporary architect I M Pei, this museum focuses on German history from ancient times onwards.
Mitte, Zeughaus, Unter den Linden 2.
Tel: (030) 203 040. Open: daily 10am–6pm. Admission charge. U-Bahn or S-Bahn to Friedrichstrasse.

Deutsches Rundfunk-Museum (German Museum of Broadcasting)

Located in a former studio at the base of the Radio Tower (Funkturm), the museum displays wirelesses from the 1920s and 1930s, and a reconstructed radio shop from the same period. Visitors may take the lift in the tower to the observation platform (138m/453ft) for dizzying views over Charlottenburg.
Masurenallee 8–74. Tel: (030) 302 8186.
Open: Wed–Mon 10am–5pm.
Admission charge. S-Bahn to Westkreuz.
Buses: 104, 149 & 219.

Deutsches Technikmuseum (German Museum of Technology)

As the giant mural on the Landwehr Canal promises, this is an Aladdin's cave for anyone with an interest in steam trains, biplanes, vintage cars, bicycles, sailing ships, and all kinds of industrial machinery and paraphernalia. With its accent on hands-on experience, the science museum is also ideal for children, but be warned – the collection can be overwhelming, so it's best to concentrate on areas of greatest appeal. The museum has the perfect home – long-abandoned industrial buildings, including the former workshops and locomotive sheds of the old Anhalter Bahnhof, Berlin's southern railway terminus, built in 1840 but demolished in the 1950s (part of the ruined façade can still be seen across the river on the corner of Schöneberger Strasse).

The ground-floor exhibits include historic aircraft such as the 1917 Fokker triplane and 1941 Junkers Ju 52; vintage cars in pristine condition, among them models designed by pioneers Gottlieb Daimler and Karl Benz; buses, motor-cycles and a 1904 fire engine. The Versuchsfeld (experiment room) offers the chance to operate buttons and gadgets, while programmed computers play chess or music. The old locomotive sheds house the steam trains, coaches, turntables and scale models. Upstairs, in the former manager's office, are models of the first German iron and steel ships, as well as locks and bridges.

There is a period café and a bookshop with postcards of old Berlin for sale.
Kreuzberg, Trebbiner Strasse 9. Tel: (030) 902 540. www.dtmb.de. Open: Tue–Fri 9am–5.30pm, Sat–Sun 10am–6pm. Admission charge. U-Bahn to Möckernbrücke or Gleisdreieck. Bus: 129.

Dokumentationszentrum Berliner Mauer (Berlin Wall Documentation Centre)

All about the infamous barrier, including accounts of attempted (and occasionally successful) East-to-West tunnel escapes beneath walled-off Bernauer Strasse. Provides maps for relevant tours of the vicinity.
Mitte, Bernauer Strasse 111. Tel: (030) 464 1030. Open: Mon–Sat 10am–5pm. Admission charge. U-Bahn to Bernauer Strasse or S-Bahn to Nordbahnhof.

East Side Gallery

Pre-unification, anti-establishment graffiti galore on a continuous 0.8km ($^1/_2$-mile) remnant of the Berlin Wall flanking an east-side canal. The multi-coloured spatterings combine angry defiance and dark humour; some are quite artistic.
Friedrichshain, Mühlenstrasse. U-Bahn to Warschauer Strasse or S-Bahn to Ostbahnhof.

Ephraim Palais

This finely restored rococo mansion (*see map, p105*) with its distinctive golden balconies and sculpted cherubic figures was built in 1766 for the court banker and jeweller to Frederick the Great, Nathan Ephraim. The architect was Friedrich Wilhelm Dietrichs. The original owner's Jewish origins made the building a target for the Nazis, who wished to widen the adjoining road. The present reconstruction, which preserves Dietrichs' façade, is slightly removed from the original site. On the first floor a museum exhibits maps and paintings from the 17th to the 19th century and is worth visiting just to see the interior of the house. The ground-floor restaurant specialises in German cuisine.
Mitte, Poststrasse 16. Tel: (030) 240 02121. Open: Tue–Sun 10am–6pm. Admission charge (Wed free). U-Bahn or

S-Bahn to Alexanderplatz. Buses: 100, 142, 147, 257 & 348.

Fernsehturm

Like it or not, the immense, thrusting television tower, complete with globe and red-and-white striped pole, is one of Berlin's most distinctive landmarks, opened in 1969. Rising to 368m (1,207ft), the Fernsehturm is considerably higher than the Eiffel Tower, and the views, on a clear day, can be spectacular. There are two vantage points: the viewing platform on the top floor or the Tele-Café.
Mitte, Alexanderplatz.
Tel: (030) 242 3333.
www.berlinerfernsehturm.de.
Open: (viewing platform) Tue–Sun 10am–6pm. Admission charge.
U-Bahn or S-Bahn to Friedrichstrasse. S-Bahn to Hackescher Markt or Oranienburger Strasse. Buses: 100, 200 & 348 to Lustgarten.

Filmmuseum Berlin – Deutsche Kinemathek

The Film Museum houses the Marlene Dietrich Collection (*see map, p96*). The permanent exhibition includes showrooms about German classics like Robert Wiene's *The Cabinet of Dr Caligari* or Fritz Lang's *Metropolis* as well as the famous artificial creatures by Ray Harryhausen. Sketches, scenery designs, models and countless exhibits document developments in German film from 1919 to the present.
Potsdamer Strasse 2. Tel: (030) 309 030. www.filmmuseum-berlin.de. Open: Tue–Sun 10am–6pm, Thur 10am–8pm. Admission charge. U-Bahn or S-Bahn to Potsdamer Platz.

The ultimate vantage point – Berlin's 368-m (1,207-ft) high Fernsehturm

Französischer Dom (French Cathedral)

On the northern side of the Gendarmenmarkt, the French Cathedral was intended for the Huguenot community, invited to Berlin by the Great Elector following the revocation of the Edict of Nantes (1685), which had guaranteed religious tolerance to French Protestants. Its distinctive tower was added between 1780 and 1785 by Karl von Gontard. The small museum of Huguenot history in the base of the

tower honours these hardworking people who played a major role in the Prussian manufacturing industry. Climb to the gallery for fine views of the square and to hear the carillon.
Mitte, Gendarmenmarkt. Tel: (030) 229 1760. Museum open: Tue–Thur & Sat noon–5pm, Sun 1–5pm. Viewing platform open: Tue–Sat 10am–4pm. Carillon chimes daily at noon, 3pm & 7pm. Free admission (admission charge for Huguenot museum). U-Bahn to Französische Strasse.

Friedrichs-Werdersche-Kirche (Schinkel Museum)

This finely proportioned red-brick church with twin towers (*see map, p99*) was designed by Schinkel (*see pp44–5*) between 1824 and 1830 in the late Gothic style. It was severely damaged during World War II but restored in the 1980s as a museum honouring Schinkel and his contemporaries. There are sculptures in the nave by Schadow, Rauch and Tieck, and the wooden gallery chronicles Schinkel's major achievements, such as the Schauspielhaus, the original Berliner Dom and the Altes Museum.
Mitte, Werderstrasse. Tel: (030) 208 1323. www.smb.museum. Open: daily 10am–6pm. Admission charge. U-Bahn or S-Bahn to Friedrichstrasse.

Gedenkstätte Deutscher Widerstand (Memorial to German Resistance)

This is where Admiral von Tirpitz planned the expansion of the German navy before World War I and Hitler made his famous *Lebensraum* speech about the German need for 'living space' (*see map, p96*). In 1944, the building, known then as the Bendlerblock, became the nerve centre for the conspiracy against Hitler led by Colonel Count Claus Schenk von Stauffenberg. When Hitler survived the bomb blast in the command centre at Rastenburg on 20 July 1944, the plot disintegrated. Stauffenberg and three of his colleagues were taken into the courtyard and shot. The other, less fortunate, conspirators were taken to Plötzensee prison, where they were tortured then hanged with piano wire,

(*Cont. on p54*)

Karl von Gontard's distinctive tower crowns the Französischer Dom

Spy capital

It was after World War II, when Berlin became, in John Le Carré's words, 'the world capital of the Cold War', that the city acquired its reputation for espionage, intrigue and double-dealing. By the early 1950s as many as 12,000 Berliners were earning at least a part-time living from selling secrets to the 'other side'. Money, not ideology, was the main motivating factor: one witness later recalled how 'a few dollars were enough to make many of the boys change sides between cups of coffee'. Defections, kidnappings and mysterious disappearances were an everyday occurrence. It did not matter that the information acquired was generally of a trivial nature. Intrigue is addictive and the rival intelligence organisations lived for the day when they would uncover that elusive military secret. And occasionally they did.

Operation Gold (fictionalised in Ian McEwan's novel *The Innocent*) was the most ingenious and ultimately the most futile enterprise of the early Cold War period. This involved tunnelling under the Soviet sector of the city to enable Western engineers

Checkpoint Charlie is now only a tourist attraction

The US Army's historic sign

to tap the telephone cables linking East Berlin with the Soviet Union and the countries of Eastern Europe. The cost, $25 million, would have been considered prohibitive in any other era, and it was not money well spent. It turned out that the master spy George Blake had let the Russians in on the secret from the start.

With the construction of the Wall and the growing East–West tensions that resulted, the stakes became higher and potentially lethal, providing writers with endless scenarios for dramatic spy novels, inspiring films such as *Funeral in Berlin* (adapted from Len Deighton's novel) and Carol Reed's thriller *The Man Between*. This is the twilight world that John Le Carré has made his own, a world where intelligence officers with all the paraphernalia of surveillance – telescopes, binoculars, directional microphones – squint into the cold night air waiting for a defector to cross the arc-lit bridge to freedom while the Vopo sharpshooters await their orders.

the proceedings being filmed for Hitler's perverted gratification.

A wreath in the courtyard marks the spot where Stauffenberg and his friends were executed, and on the second floor an exhibition charts the history of German resistance. Every oppositionist organisation is credited, from youth groups like the White Rose to trade unionists, Communists and Social Democrats, churchmen and women, Jews and workers. The Bendlerblock has recently been returned to the Defence Ministry amid some controversy.

Tiergarten, Stauffenbergstrasse 13–14. Tel: (030) 269 95000. www.gdw-berlin.de. Open: Mon–Fri 9am–6pm (Thur 9am–8pm), Sat–Sun 10am–6pm. Free admission. U-Bahn to Kurfürstenstrasse. Bus: 129 to Stauffenbergstrasse.

Monument to victims at Plötzensee

Gedenkstätte Plötzensee (Plötzensee Memorial)

In the grounds of the gloomy prison building, now a remand centre for juveniles, is a paved courtyard with a memorial wall bearing the inscription: 'To the victims of the Hitler dictatorship 1933–1945'. A white urn contains soil samples from each concentration camp.

More than 2,500 people died here in the most brutal circumstances. The twin brick buildings behind the wall were the 'death house' and execution chamber. The hooks from which the July plotters against Hitler were hanged have been preserved, the only relics of a nightmarish past. An exhibition of photographs includes death warrants and, even more eerie, the invitation card to an execution. A leaflet in English is available on request.

Charlottenburg, Hüttigpfad. Tel: (030) 344 3226. www.gedenkstaette-ploetzensee.de. Open: daily, Mar–Oct 9am–5pm; Nov–Feb 9am–4pm. Free admission. Bus: 123 from S-Bahnhof Tiergarten.

Gendarmenmarkt

Once the site of a bustling market, the Gendarmenmarkt is named after an infantry regiment which was stationed here in the 18th century. (In the Communist era the square was known as Platz der Akademie.) Like neighbouring Bebelplatz, the existing layout of the square dates from the period of Frederick the Great and

Schinkel's Konzerthaus dominates the Gendarmenmarkt

testifies to the contemporary obsession with making an 'Athens on the Spree'. In this case, however, the model is Rome's Piazza del Popolo. Three architectural masterpieces overlook the square: the German and French Cathedrals (*see pp47–8 & 50–51*), and Schinkel's Schauspielhaus (*see p98*), completed in 1821, recently renamed the Konzerthaus.

Outside the theatre a statue of Friedrich Schiller commemorates the great playwright's celebrated visit to Berlin in 1804, shortly before his death. It is a mark of Schiller's stature that German drama is, for the most part, performed on the square today and not the French comedies so assiduously promoted by Frederick the Great. However, the playwright most closely associated with Berlin, Heinrich von Kleist (*see panel, p56*), has no memorial here. Another literary connection with the square is the writer E T A Hoffmann, whose fantastic stories inspired Offenbach's *Tales of Hoffmann.* A famous restaurant, Lutter und Wegener, was the author's favourite haunt.

Mitte. U-Bahn to Französische Strasse.

Glienicker Brücke and Schloss Glienicke

This unremarkable bridge across the Havel once marked the frontier between East and West and was the scene of dramatic spy swaps, notably the exchange, in 1962, of a Soviet agent for the US U-2 pilot Francis Gary Powers, who was shot down over Russia on a reconnaissance mission. The trade

Italianate Schloss Glienicke with splendid views across the River Havel

in human hostages, one of the harsher symptoms of the Cold War, seems a profanity in this idyllic natural setting. Protocol on such occasions demanded that representatives of both camps approach one another from their respective ends of the bridge, making towards a white painted line in the centre. Both prisoners had then to cross the border simultaneously. Meanwhile, plain-clothes intelligence agents, diplomats, and military figures with binoculars eyed the proceedings intently, watching for any trick or slip-up. The moment the prisoner made physical contact with someone from his own side, he was deemed to be safe.

The Glienicke Bridge has long been of strategic importance. In 1945 it was blown up by advancing Soviet forces and subsequently rebuilt by the East German government, which, either with calculated cynicism or indifference to irony, renamed it the Unity Bridge.

Set back from the road on the Wannsee bank is the Schloss Glienicke, a serene Italianate villa guarded by a pair of golden lions. It was built by

HEINRICH VON KLEIST (1777–1811)

One of the most celebrated German Romantic writers, as much for the manner of his death as for his stories and plays, Kleist was brought up in the Prussian military tradition which he later unceremoniously rejected. His portrayal of the army in the play *The Prince of Homburg* made him a particular *bête noire* of Frederick William III, who outlawed his work, condemning him to a life of poverty. Ultimately driven to despair, he and his friend Henriette Vogel came to the wooded slopes of Wannsee and fulfilled a previously agreed suicide pact. Kleist's reputation was made overnight!

Schinkel in 1826 for the brother of Kaiser William I. The palace is closed to the public, but not the gardens, which were landscaped by the same Peter Lenné who designed both the park at Sanssouci and the Tiergarten. The gardens offer superb views of the Havel and the surrounding woodland, and contain a number of delightful arcadian follies, including a teahouse, rotunda and mock cloister, part of the fabric of which comes from a monastery in Venice. There is a restaurant with an outside terrace.
Zehlendorf, Königstrasse 36. Free entry to grounds. Bus: 116.

Hackesche Höfe

Much-visited and much-photographed, an altogether sensational restoration of eight interconnected courtyards conceived in 1905–7. Walls covered with glazed blue mosaics typ[...] *Jugendstil* design bravado. P[...] include a café, artists' studio[...] Chamäleon Varieté cabaret (*see p149*).
Mitte, Rosenthaler Strasse. U-Bahn to Weinmeister Strasse or S-Bahn to Hackescher Markt.

Hamburger Bahnhof Museum für Gegenwart (Museum of the Present)

The museum in a former railway station is a must-see for its exterior light installation by Dan Flavin. The permanent exhibition includes works by Andy Warhol, Joseph Beuys (with a video archive of his performances) and Anselm Kiefer. There is an excellent art bookshop. Look out for events and performances.
Tiergarten, Invalidenstrasse 50–51. Tel: (030) 397 8340.

Hackesche Höfe was restored and extended after the fall of the Berlin Wall

www.hamburgerbahnhof.de. Open: Tue–Fri 10am–6pm (Thur 10am–10pm), Sat–Sun 11am–6pm. Admission charge. S-Bahn to Hauptbahnhof.

Hansaviertel

This much-vaunted housing development was the showpiece of the 1957 International Building Exhibition. More than 50 architects from all over the world contributed to the project, including the founder of the Bauhaus, Walter Gropius. The intention was to rejuvenate the northwestern edge of the Tiergarten, which had been devastated during World War II. The estate consists of a series of modest tower blocks and apartment buildings with conventional amenities (church, shops, nursery, etc) and set in a landscaped environment. Once at the architectural cutting edge, it now looks distinctly dated.
Tiergarten, Altonaer Strasse.
U-Bahn to Hansaplatz.

Part of the world-renowned Hansaviertel housing project

Haus am Checkpoint Charlie

The museum to the Berlin Wall is a stone's throw away from the famous crossing point where Soviet and American tanks once confronted each other. The prefabricated hut which served as a border post has been moved to the Deutsches Technikmuseum (*see pp48–9*), but you can still see the red and white barrier and the sign in four languages warning that 'You are leaving the American Sector'. The museum charts the history of the Wall, but the emphasis is on escapology, the exhibits including hot-air balloons, cars with specially concealed compartments, and other ephemera. While fun in an off-beat way, the museum appears vacuous, bearing in mind the tragic implications for the people of Berlin. Outside, an area fenced off by metal railings contains Wall paraphernalia, including sentry posts and rolls of barbed wire. It is also possible to buy pieces of Wall here, but be warned: there are as many slabs of 'Wall' doing the rounds as there were pieces of the 'true' cross in the Middle Ages.
Kreuzberg, Friedrichstrasse 44.
Tel: (030) 253 7250.
www.mauer-museum.de.
Open: daily 9am–10pm. Admission charge. U-Bahn to Kochstrasse.

Berliners affectionately call the Haus der Kulturen der Welt the 'pregnant oyster'

Haus der Kulturen der Welt (House of World Cultures)

Berliners call this testament to German–US friendship the 'pregnant oyster', after the yawning cantilevered roof; in fact, the architecture is meant to suggest the awnings of tents – funfairs and sideshows were held here in the past, and Tent Street (In den Zelten) is just around the corner. Like a tent in the wind, Hugh Stubbins' roof collapsed in 1980 and had to be replaced. There are a number of sculptures in the garden, most notably *Large Butterfly* by Henry Moore. The building, originally known as the Kongresshalle, stages temporary exhibitions.

Tiergarten, John-Foster-Dulles-Allee 10. Tel: (030) 397 870. Open: Tue–Thur 2–6pm, Fri–Sun 10am–8pm. Bus: 100 to Haus der Kulturen der Welt.

Jüdisches Museum (Jewish Museum)

This is the most visited museum in Germany at present. A visit is a memorable and uplifting experience. Polish-born architect Daniel Libeskind created a lasting, timeless monument to Jewish history and life in Berlin and Germany. The spectacularly conceived zinc building, based on the historical and emotional parameters of the Holocaust, deserves a guided tour in

itself for a fuller appreciation of the scale of vision and inspiration from which it stems. As an aesthetic and emotional package, it does not get much better than this. The entrance of the former Berlin-Museum now leads to the Jüdisches Museum.
Kreuzberg, Lindenstrasse 9–14. Tel: (030) 259 93300. www.jmberlin.de. Open: Mon 10am–10pm; Tue–Sun 10am–8pm. Admission charge. U-Bahn to Hallesches Tor. Bus: 265.

Kaiser Wilhelm Gedächtniskirche (Kaiser William Memorial Church)

Only the blackened shell remains of this intended memorial to Kaiser William I, built in neo-Romanesque style between 1891 and 1895 by Franz Schwechten, which was bombed on the night of 22 November 1943. Its ruin has been preserved to commemorate the futility of war. An exhibition of photographs in the portico develops the theme. The ruined tower contrasts with two modern stained-glass buildings which reflect it, a bell tower and an octagonal chapel with a strikingly beautiful interior. Berlin wits call the blackened ruin the 'jagged tooth', the chapel the 'make-up box' and the tower the 'lipstick tube'.
Charlottenburg, Breitscheidplatz. Tel: (030) 218 5023. Open: daily 9am–7pm. Memorial Hall open: Tue–Sat 10am–5pm. Free admission. U-Bahn or S-Bahn to Zoologischer Garten. U-Bahn to Kurfürstendamm.

The zinc-faced Jewish Museum is a masterpiece of modern architecture

Karl-Marx-Allee

A 1½km- (1-mile-) long boulevard (originally named Stalinallee), made extra-wide for socialist-orchestrated parades when laid out half a century ago, lined with the era's 'workers' paradise' housing blocks. It is strangely fascinating as a surviving example of the DDR's fixation on pompous Soviet-inspired neoclassical urban planning. This is where angry construction workers began the 17 June 1953 uprising (*see* Bundesministerium der Finanzen, *p39*). There is extensive documentation in Café Sybelle.

Friedrichshain. Café Sybelle, Karl-Marx-Allee 72. Open: daily 10am–8pm. U-Bahn to Schillingstrasse & Strausberger Platz.

Käthe-Kollwitz-Museum

The life and work of the committed social artist Käthe Kollwitz (1867–1945) are celebrated here. The setting, a handsome early 20th-century mansion in Charlottenburg, is hardly appropriate, bearing in mind that Kollwitz was moved to paint by the misery and hardship she observed in working-class Prenzlauer Berg, where her husband was a doctor. After she lost a son during World War I, the nightmare of war became an additional preoccupation that was reflected in her work.

Kollwitz's socialist ideals did not endear her to the Nazis; her work was banned in 1936 and she was compelled to leave her post at the Academy of Arts. She died near Dresden a few days before the end of World War II.

The museum consists of paintings, woodcuts, charcoal drawings and sculptures created by Kollwitz during a prolific artistic career. The subjects are almost uniformly melancholic, but their underlying integrity makes them profoundly moving.

Her studies of women emphasise collective strength in the face of unbearable hardship, as can clearly be seen in the sculpture *Muttergruppe*. The striking poster *Nie Wieder Krieg* (*Never Again War*) and the cycle of woodcuts, both of which commemorate the death of her son Peter, strongly reflect her strong belief and lifelong dedication to pacifism.

Charlottenburg, Fasanenstrasse 24. Tel: (030) 882 5210. www.kaethe-kollwitz.de. Open: Wed–Mon 11am–6pm. Admission charge. U-Bahn to Kurfürstendamm.

Kennedy Museum

This museum (*see map, p99*) pays tribute to US President John F Kennedy, who made a memorable visit to Berlin in June 1963, during the Cold War era. Exhibits include documents, news reports and many photographs, plus personal belongings such as JFK's black Hermès attaché case and one of Jacqueline Kennedy's signature pillbox hats.

Mitte, Pariser Platz 4a. Tel: (030) 206 53570. Open: daily 10am–6pm. Admission charge. U-Bahn to Brandenburger Tor or S-Bahn to Pariser Platz.

Köpenick district

There continue to be frenzied attempts to restore this attractive old town at the confluence of the Dahme and Spree rivers, the fabric of which was allowed to deteriorate by the East German government. Take a tolerant view, and you will find much charm here.

To get to the old town, either take tram 86 or walk along Bahnhofstrasse, turning left at the junction with Lindenstrasse. Pass the park on the left and cross the Damm Bridge, where the River Dahme takes leave of the Spree. Köpenick received its charter in the 13th century when it was already a thriving market town and fishing village. The red brick, neo-Gothic building, with an impressive tower, is the Rathaus (Town Hall). The town acquired a sizeable factory suburb in the 19th century. Köpenick's workers fiercely resisted the Nazi takeover in 1933 and suffered for this in the Köpenicker Blutwoche (Week of Blood), when over 90 Communists and Social Democrats were murdered.

Schloss Köpenick

Immediately beyond the old town is Schloss Köpenick. There has been a fortress here since the 9th century when the Slavs began colonising the area. The present building is Dutch Baroque and was built in 1681 for the son of the Great Elector by Rutger van Langefelt. It now houses a small museum of decorative arts (Kunstgewerbemuseum Schloss Köpenick). More noteworthy is the Wappensaal, with its exquisite stuccoed ceiling, the work of the Italian Giovanni Carove, and the beautifully restored chapel, designed by Arnold Nering in 1685.

Tel: (030) 266 2931. Open: Tue–Fri 10am–6pm, Sat–Sun 11am–6pm. Admission charge. S-Bahn to Köpenick, then tram 62 or 68 to Schlossinsel.

Kulturforum

This sprawling complex of museums and concert halls on the southern edge of the Tiergarten was conceived by Hans Scharoun in the early 1960s. The buildings are grouped rather randomly around an isolated red-and-white brick church. This is the St Mattäus-Kirche, designed in Italian Byzantine style by August Stüler in 1844–6, sole survivor of a once fashionable neighbourhood whose high-society residents were described in the novels of Theodor Fontane.

During the 1930s, Hitler cleared much of the area as part of his plans for a grandiose North–South Axis running from near the Brandenburg Gate. Most of the former diplomatic quarter was removed, the exceptions being the Italian and Japanese embassies – now the Japanese–German Center.

Of the modern buildings, the most eye-catching is the Philharmonie, with its eccentric angles and gold cladding. The interior of the concert hall, home of the Berlin Philharmonic Orchestra, is well known for the excellent quality of its acoustics.

The Kulturforum is also home to the Kammermusiksaal (Chamber Concert Hall) and Staatsbibliothek (National Library), the Museum of Musical Instruments (*see p66*), the New National Gallery (*see pp67–8*) and the Museum of Applied Art (*see pp64–5*).

Since 1996, many valuable collections in the new Gemäldegalerie (*see below*) and Kupferstichkabinett (*see pp65–6*) have been amassed from museums all over Berlin.

Gemäldegalerie (Picture Gallery)

The new building for the picture gallery of the Staatliche Museen Berlin opened in 1998. Situated in the Kulturforum, it offers approximately 7,000sq m (75,350sq ft) of space in 53 rooms, and combines the displays that had been housed in the Gemäldegaler and in the Gemäldegalerie Museum on Museum Island s division of Germany.

The Picture Gallery has one of the world's finest collections of European art from the 13th to the 18th century. The bulk of the collection, founded in 1830, was acquired in the 19th century and systematically built up and perfected.

The octagonal Rembrandt room enjoys a key position at the heart of the museum. The 16 works displayed form one of the largest and most splendid collections of the artist's work in the world. Other masters of Dutch Baroque whose works can be enjoyed here are Frans Hals, Rubens, Vermeer and Van Dyck.

The main hall of the Gemäldegalerie

Other highlights of the collection include an altarpiece by the Master of the Darmstadt Passion, an anonymous artist whose association with this work led art historians to refer to him by a descriptive name. There is also a magnificent sequence of portraits by Dürer and Hans Holbein. Even more rewarding is the Flemish primitive art, beautifully composed, rich in symbolism, and with a wealth of topographical detail. All the great masters are represented here, from Campin and Van Eyck – including the exquisite *Madonna in the Church* – to Petrus Christus and Rogier van der Weyden. There are leaflets in English explaining Pieter Bruegel the Elder's wonderfully inventive *Netherlandish Proverbs* (1559), which wittily illustrate sayings like 'He who has spilled his porridge cannot scrape it all up again'.

The earthy uninhibitedness of Bruegel is in stark contrast to the restrained elegance of the 18th-century English and French artists, who include Watteau, Gainsborough, Grueze and Boucher. The Italian collection, while represented by some great names – Masaccio, Fra Angelico, Botticelli, Bellini, Raphael, Titian and Tintoretto – is not of outstanding quality.

Tiergarten, Matthäikirchplatz 4–6. www.smb.museum. Open: Tue–Sun 10am–6pm. Admission charge. U-Bahn or S-Bahn to Potsdamer Platz. Buses: 129, 148, 200, 341 & 348.

Kunstgewerbemuseum (Museum of Decorative Arts)

This ugly modern red-brick building conceals a fine collection and a brilliant display. It was founded in 1867 and contains the bulk of the pre-war national collection of applied art. (The remainder is in Schloss Köpenick.)

Looking across Potsdamer Platz towards the Philharmonie

NEARBY

Bauhaus-Archiv, Gedenkstätte Deutscher Widerstand, Filmmuseum at Sony Center.

At the entrance level, there is an information gallery where craft methods are explained in their historical context, a cafeteria and shop. In chronological sequence, the museum begins one level below with a rich display of crosses, stained glass, caskets and ornate reliquaries, dating from medieval and Renaissance times. What makes the collection unique are the works of the medieval goldsmiths: the Dionysius Treasure of Enger-Herford, which includes an exquisitely bejewelled 8th-century Burse reliquary said to have been produced for Charlemagne, and the 'Guelph Cross', part of the former treasure of the church of St Blasius, Braunschweig. Equally impressive are the baptismal bowl crafted for the Emperor Frederick Barbarossa and a 15th-century reliquary of St George slaying the dragon. On the same floor are Brussels tapestries, Venetian glass, Nuremberg silverware and Florentine majolica. The Lüneburg Town Hall Silver Plate (Lüneburger Ratssilber), dating from the 15th and 16th centuries, evokes the wealth of this distinguished Hanseatic port.

The collection resumes on the top floor with impressive displays of glass, silver, porcelain, stoneware, pewter and ivory. Perhaps the most interesting item here is the contents of the Pommersche Kunstschrank, an ebony cabinet destroyed by fire during World War II. Stuffed into the secret drawers and niches was a potpourri of precious objects, including surgical instruments, hairbrushes, games and miniature books, all made in Augsburg for the Duke of Pommern-Stettin in the early 17th century. The 18th-century porcelain is also worth seeing, especially Konrad Linck's grouping of Meleager and Atalante, produced in Frankenthal in 1778. All the major workshops are represented, among them Meissen, Nymphenburg and the Royal Porcelain Manufacturers of Berlin (KPM). Bringing the exhibition into the 20th century are sections devoted to *Jugendstil*/Art Nouveau glass and ceramics and Art Deco.

An entertaining counterpoint to the craftsmanship of past ages is the display of modern domestic items in the basement, proving that even lowly objects such as typewriters, telephones, kettles and hairdryers can be aesthetically pleasing.

Herbert-von-Karajan-Strasse. Tel: (030) 266 2902/3. www.smb.museum. Open: Tue–Fri 10am–6pm, Sat–Sun 11am–6pm. Admission charge. U-Bahn or S-Bahn to Potsdamer Platz. Buses: 29, 41, 48, 85, 200 & 347.

Kupferstichkabinett (Museum of Prints and Drawings)

This is a small museum of prints, drawings and engravings, much of it of high quality, amounting to 80,000

and 520,000 printed
Among the artists
Dürer, Botticelli,
, Rembrandt, Goya, and
Kandinsky, Picasso and
Otto Dix.

Tiergarten, Matthäikirchplatz 8. Exhibition open: Tue–Fri 10am–6pm, Sat–Sun 11am–6pm. Studiensaal: Tel: (030) 266 2002. www.smb.museum. Open: Tue–Fri 9am–4pm. U-Bahn or S-Bahn to Potsdamer Platz. Buses: 129, 148, 200, 248, 341 & 348.

Musikinstrumenten-Museum (Museum of Musical Instruments)

Tucked away behind the Philharmonie is the often neglected Museum of Musical Instruments, a branch of the Institute for Musical Research. The building was designed by Edgar Wisniewski in the early 1980s and is ideally suited to its purpose. Instruments are imaginatively laid out in spacious, well-lit galleries and are almost too accessible – avoid the temptation to touch, which immediately sets off an alarm! Altogether there are more than 2,200 items in the collection and each is lovingly maintained by the Institute's craft department. Though one of the staff will occasionally give a demonstration, it is also possible to listen to sample performances on banks of headphones situated next to the display cases.

The range of instruments is comprehensive – everything from ancient bagpipes, complete with animal bladders, to Stradivarius violins, and the latest computer wizardry. There are harpsichords and claviers, each individually carved and painted, pianos of Beethoven vintage from the Berlin workshops of Kisting and Stöcker – including one with a double keyboard – and a Silbermann pianoforte similar to the one J S Bach played for Frederick the Great at Potsdam in 1747. A skilled musician himself, Frederick kept the instrument makers in business for more than 40 years; two transverse flutes from his personal collection are on permanent display. In the early 19th century, Berlin was a world leader in the manufacture of wind instruments. In 1818 production began of brass instruments with valves – an innovation which added immeasurably to the range and precision of horns, trumpets and trombones. The world's first bass tuba was also built in Berlin in 1835 by Johann Gottfried Moritz. The prize for the most bizarre contraption must go to the Orchestron, an enormous one-man-band of an organ kitted out with cymbals, drums, glockenspiel and whatever else the inventor could come up with.

Tiergarten, Matthäikirchplatz at Kulturforum (Tiergartenstrasse 1). Tel: (030) 254 811. www.mim-berlin.de. Open: Tue–Fri 9am–5pm (Thur 9am–10pm), Sat–Sun 10am–5pm. Admission charge. U-Bahn or S-Bahn to Potsdamer Platz. Buses: 129, 142, 148, 248, 341 & 348.

Neue Nationalgalerie (New National Gallery)

The orientation of this challenging exhibition is towards international modern art, although 19th-century French and German painting is also well represented. *The Archer*, a sculpture in the garden by Henry Moore, sets the tone. Mies van der Rohe, a director of the Bauhaus who fled to the USA in 1938, designed the building with the distinctive black canopy, which, back in the 1960s, was regarded as being in the vanguard of modernism. About half the museum space is taken up with temporary exhibitions, for which there is an extra charge. Some of these shows are spectacular, so check with tourist information o listings magazines.

One of the gallery's mos features is its roominess – i designed with large canvases in mind. Wander through and admire the work of some of the leading artists of the post-war era, including Roy Lichtenstein, Robert Rauschenberg, Frank Stella and Joseph Beuys. But don't ignore the new generation of painters: Gerhard Richter's *Atelier* and Richard Lindner's witty *Arizona Girl* are a reminder that modern art can be stimulating and entertaining, as well as thought-provoking.

Step back in time by visiting the lower floor, where the focus is on French and German painting from

Mies van der Rohe's Neue Nationalgalerie was opened in 1968

..e 19th and early 20th centuries. The most distinguished artists here are Adolph Menzel, Arnold Böcklin, Max Beckmann, George Grosz and Otto Dix. Look out for Menzel's *Das Flötenkonzert* (*The Flute Concert*), a charming portrait of Frederick the Great playing the flute at Sanssouci; Böcklin's morose *Die Toteninsel* (*Island of the Dead*), and one of Grosz's most savage satires, *Pillars of Society.* The French school encompasses works from the Impressionists to Matisse: Monet's *St Germain l'Auxerrois* and Manet's *In the Winter Garden* are worth seeking out.

New to the collection is Ernst Ludwig Kirchner's *Potsdamer Platz*, painted in 1914, which stands in fascinating contrast to the contemporary Platz situated just a few metres away. Kirchner painted his scene of Berlin nightlife shortly after the beginning of World War I.

American artist Jenny Holzer's installation *HO*, comprising digital thin bases along the ceiling, was kept on here after an exhibition of her work in 2002. Poems, slogans and sayings run freely along the digital strips perforating the transparent walls of the museum, combining lightness and geometry.

If your legs are giving out by this time, stop off at the Café Buchhandlung, which serves hot meals as well as light refreshment.

In addition to the permanent exhibition, the Neue Nationalgalerie specialises in changing shows of modern art such as the highly successful Picasso retrospective in 2006. *Potsdamer Strasse 50. Tel: (030) 266 2650/1/3/4. www.smb.museum. Open: Tue–Fri 10am–6pm (Thur 10am–10pm), Sat–Sun 11am–6pm. Admission charge. U-Bahn or S-Bahn to Potsdamer Platz.*

Ludwig-Erhard-Haus

This radically postmodern structure's 15 gigantic metallic arches promptly inspired wisecracking locals to nickname it the 'Armadillo' upon completion a decade ago. In a more conservative vein, Berlin's Stock Exchange and Chamber of Commerce function inside. Visitors have access to skylit lobby areas and two atria. *Charlottenburg, Fasanenstrasse 83–4. Tel: (030) 723 90157. Open: Mon–Fri 8am–6pm. Free admission. U-Bahn to Ernst-Reuter-Platz or Uhlandstrasse.*

Marienkirche

The second-oldest church in Berlin after the Nikolaikirche is a miraculous survivor of the heaviest bombing raid on the city, which occurred on the morning of 3 February 1945. Even more remarkable is the survival of the tower which had previously been destroyed by fire on no fewer than five occasions. The existing red-brick structure is 15th-century German Gothic, while the present tower, with its distinctive lantern extension, dates from 1790 and is the work of Carl Gotthard Langhans, better known as the architect of the

Brandenburg Gate. The interior is spacious, if a little shabby. Particularly noteworthy is the ornate Baroque pulpit by Andreas Schlüter (1703). Near the tower is the *Totentanz* or *Dance of Death*, a medieval wall painting 22.6m (74ft) long, commemorating an outbreak of plague in 1484. J S Bach played the organ in the Marienkirche in 1747, and today there are free recitals every Tuesday and Thursday at 2.30pm for 20 minutes.
Mitte, Neuer Markt. Tel: (030) 242 4467. Open: Mon–Thur 10am–noon & 1–5pm, Sat noon–4pm. Free admission. U-Bahn or S-Bahn to Alexanderplatz. Buses: 100, 157 & 348.

Designed in the 19th century, the façade of the Martin-Gropius-Bau is in Italian Renaissance style

Martin-Gropius-Bau

Designed in the style of the Italian Renaissance, this building dates from 1881 and is the work of Martin Gropius, uncle of Walter, founder of the Bauhaus movement. The interior is spacious and lavish, a courtyard covered by a glass dome, with gilded arcades, richly decorated ceilings, mosaics and chandeliers. Some really extraordinary exhibitions are held here.
Kreuzberg, Stresemannstrasse 110. Tel: (030) 254 860. Open: Tue–Sun 10am–8pm. Admission charge. U-Bahn or S-Bahn to Potsdamer Platz.

Mitte district

The Mitte, literally 'middle', is the historic centre of Berlin. The twin medieval settlements of Berlin-Cölln grew up on the banks of the Spree near Museum Island. The town gradually extended to include the Nikolaiviertel and the neighbourhood of the Marienkirche. Beginning in the 17th century, the old fortifications were torn down and replaced with squares and gardens, while three new suburbs were added: Friedrichswerder, Dorotheenstadt and Friedrichstadt. In the period of renewed confidence following the defeat of Napoleon, the city was embellished with fine neoclassical buildings, many the work of Berlin's greatest architect, Karl Friedrich Schinkel. After World War I, the westward expansion of the city accelerated, but Friedrichstrasse, Leipzigerstrasse and Potsdamer Platz remained important centres for business and entertainment. The Mitte was reduced to ruins by bombing during World War II – the Reich Chancellery and the Military High Command were located here. Since 1989, the Mitte has been successfully reintegrated with the West End and injected with new life.

The Berlin Philharmonic

If the players of the Berlin Philharmonic are virtuosi to a man and woman, the orchestra's fearsome reputation has derived equally from its principal conductors, all men of distinction, some of genius. Hans von Bülow, Nikisch, Furtwängler, Herbert von Karajan . . . the list reads like a roll call of the great.

Bülow, the world's first virtuoso conductor, became renowned for his flamboyance on the podium – a gift to cartoonists. His ability to conduct from memory was legendary: 'You should have the score in your head, not your head in the score' was his advice to a young protégé, the composer Richard Strauss. Under his successor, Arthur Nikisch, the orchestra became famous for its impassioned performances. Tchaikovsky, several of whose works he premiered, was one of many to sing his praises.

The Berlin Philharmonic's association with the gramophone began before World War I, with a recording by Bülow of Beethoven's *5th Symphony*. But it was Nikisch's successor, Wilhelm Furtwängler, who began to exploit the medium, and the Berlin Philharmonic became renowned throughout the world for its performances of Beethoven, Bruckner and Wagner. After the Nazi seizure of power in 1933, Furtwängler and his orchestra were forced to toe the ideological line. The maestro ended the war hopelessly compromised and the orchestra, too, fell from grace.

Herbert von Karajan became music director in 1955, and quickly re-established the orchestra's place on the world stage. Karajan promoted the cult of the maestro to the point where some of his critics whispered darkly about megalomania. But to Berliners, who appreciated his contribution to the revitalisation of the city's cultural life after the war, and to music lovers everywhere, Karajan's genius as a conductor was undeniable. His death in July 1989 deprived the musical world of a colossus.The orchestra has continued to be a formidable instrument in the hands of British conductor Sir Simon Rattle, whose style is more low-key than Karajan's, but no less self-assured. The cult of the maestro may be disappearing, but the signs are that the Berlin Philharmonic has once again fallen on its feet.

The Philharmonie, home of the Berlin Philharmonic Orchestra

Moabit district

The area north of the Tiergarten became a centre of industry in the mid-19th century, after the Borsig locomotive works had moved here from Kreuzberg. The tenement blocks around Beusselstrasse, though now spruced up, are a reminder of Moabit's working-class past. For Berliners, Moabit will always be associated with prisons: the jail on Turmstrasse no longer functions, but Plötzensee, notorious under the Nazis, still exists as a youth reformatory, and there is a women's prison nearby. Nowadays, industrial Moabit is confined to the area around the Westhafen docks, though even here stretches of the Spree can be surprisingly scenic.

Museum Berlin-Karlshorst

On 9 May 1945, an east-side house used as a military engineers' outpost became a historic landmark when a Wehrmacht High Command delegation led by Field Marshal Keitel arrived to sign documents of unconditional surrender – a direct prelude to the official end of World War II in Europe. Photographs and artefacts document the event.

Karlshorst, Zwieseler Strasse 4. Tel: (030) 501 50810. Open: Tues–Sun 10am–6pm. Free admission. S-Bahn to Karlshorst (line 3).

Museum für Kommunikation (Postal Museum)

An engaging display of franking machines, old mail boxes, stamps and other postal paraphernalia. The collection of prototype telephones from the late 19th century is outstanding.

Mitte, Leipziger Strasse 16. Tel: (030) 202 940. Open: Tue–Fri 9am–5pm, Sat–Sun 11am–7pm. Free admission. U-Bahn to Mohrenstrasse. Buses: 148 & 348.

Museumsinsel

Museum Island was conceived in the 1820s as a sanctum for the educated citizen to reflect on the artistic achievements of the Classical past. It was a new idea, but not one confined to Prussia – the British Museum in London dates from the same period, and Napoleon had already exhibited the plunder from his conquests to an enthusiastic public in Paris.

To house the collection, which was based on the Prussian royal family's Chamber of Antiquities, part of the Spree was drained and a Classical temple commissioned from the great architect Karl Friedrich Schinkel. But

WILHELM VON BODE 1845–1929

The curator of Museum Island for more than 20 years, Bode abandoned a career in law to become a world expert on Renaissance art. He began collecting on behalf of the German government in the 1870s, well ahead of much wealthier American institutions and private collectors Mellon and Frick. The result was a superb collection of old masters. Bode was a canny fund-raiser; private individuals were enticed into donating paintings by offers of personal introductions to the Kaiser!

Museumsinsel

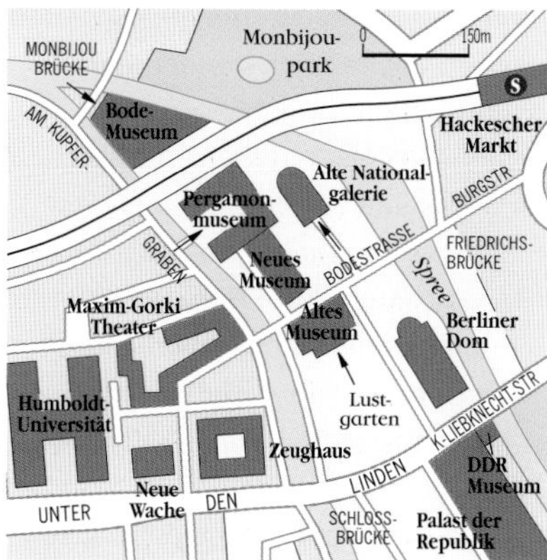

when the museum opened in 1830 the contents seemed too paltry for the monumental surroundings.

Schinkel and fellow sculptor Daniel Rauch travelled to Italy and Greece on the lookout for likely purchases. They were assisted by academics such as Wilhelm von Humboldt, who advised on the merits of the various private collections on offer. But by far the biggest contribution to the collection was made by the archaeologist Carl Richard Lepsius, who, profiting from the naïvety of the Ottoman ruler of Egypt, amassed a hoard of treasures.

There was now an embarrassment of riches and more museum space was needed. The Neues Museum was opened in 1855 and the Nationalgalerie in 1876. Spurred on by the prospect of more empty rooms and by a belief in Germany's civilising mission, the archaeologists went to work with a vengeance. Heinrich Schliemann's exciting discoveries at Troy were followed by equally rewarding excavations at Olympia in Greece and Pergamon (Bergama) in Turkey. The culmination was Robert Koldewey's expedition of 1899–1912, which uncovered the awe-inspiring treasures of Babylon. By the time the host countries were alerted to what they were losing and had begun to restrict the export of antiquities, the Germans had secured a stupendous haul.

Until the outbreak of World War II, it was possible for visitors to Berlin to review a succession of ancient civilisations simply by walking the length of Museum Island. But the war had a disastrous impact on all the Berlin collections. Many of the treasures were looted by the occupying Soviet forces and taken to Moscow, where they have only recently re-emerged. Others ended up in the hands of the Allies and are currently housed in Dahlem and Charlottenburg. Some of these collections have been merged with those of Museum Island but the logistics are formidable.

No visit to Berlin is complete without a visit to Museum Island, especially the Pergamon Museum.
Mitte. S-Bahn to Hackescher Markt or Friedrichstrasse.
Buses: 100, 157 & 348.

Alte Nationalgalerie

Designed by Friedrich August Stüler in the neoclassical style in 1867, the Nationalgalerie was established to display contemporary German art.

(A famous retrospective exhibition in 1906 introduced the German public to its rich 19th-century heritage.)

Most of the best work is now dispersed or in private hands. Nonetheless, it is worth looking out for paintings by Adolph Menzel and the collection of modern Secessionist and Expressionist art. The display varies, but you may see works by Lovis Corinth, Lesser Ury, Max Liebermann and Ernst Ludwig Kirchner.
Mitte, Bodestrasse 1–3. Tel: (030) 209 05577. www.smb.spk-berlin.de. Open: Wed–Sun 9am–6pm. Admission charge.

Altes Museum

To receive the full impact of this magnificent building it is necessary to approach it from the vast, tree-colonnaded space of the Lustgarten. One of Schinkel's great masterpieces, the Altes Museum is his homage to Classical architecture and a powerful reminder of his vision of Berlin as 'Athens on the Spree'. The visitor encounters a façade 87m (285ft) long, the expanse broken evenly by 18 massive Ionic columns supporting an entablature crowned with brooding imperial eagles and an inscription in gold lettering to Kaiser Frederick

Athens on the Spree – Berlin's neoclassical Alte Nationalgalerie

William III, who financed Berlin's first public museum.

The building took all of six years to complete and originally housed the Kaiser's modest collection of paintings and sculptures. Not content with the overwhelming impression made by the façade, Schinkel worked on a surprise in the interior: hidden in the core of the building is a Rotunda, inspired, like St-Hedwigs-Kathedrale (*see p82*), by the Pantheon in Rome. For Schinkel this was the 'sanctuary' where the most precious objects were to be revered. Statues of the gods surround the visitor between the columns on ground level and in the ambulatory above, while natural light streams in from the roof to reveal the cofferwork of the dome. The museum is currently used for major temporary exhibitions and international art shows.
Mitte, Am Lustgarten.
Tel: (030) 209 05577.
www.smb.spk-berlin.de. Special exhibitions only: Wed–Sun 9am–5pm. Admission charge.

Antikensammlung (Collection of Classical Antiquities)

This is a fabulous representation of decorative art from the ancient world, on display in the Pergamon Museum and the main floor of the Altes Museum. It consists of about half of the contents of the former Antiquarium. This was one of the Classical departments of the Prussian state museum, which unfortunately became dispersed in the chaotic aftermath of World War II.

On the ground floor, look out for the Corinthian helmet, which evokes the great confrontations between the Greeks and the Persians; also the idol from the Cycladic Islands, strikingly modern in appearance. Highlights on the first floor include the exquisitely proportioned *Amphora of the Berlin Painter*, a bust of Cleopatra, and a playful sculpture of a boy removing a thorn from his foot. In the Treasury, located on the second floor, you can see displayed a hoard of Roman silver that was discovered at Hildesheim in 1868.
Mitte, Pergamonmuseum, entrance Am Kupfergraben and Altes Museum, entrance Lustgarten. Open: Tue–Sun 10am–6pm (Thur 10am–10pm).
U-Bahn or S-Bahn to Friedrichstrasse. S-Bahn to Hackescher Markt. Buses: 100, 200, 348 to Lustgarten & 147 to Universitätsstrasse. Trams: 1, 2, 3, 4, 5, 6, 50 & 53.

Bode-Museum

The best view of this handsome building, surrounded on three sides by the River Spree, is from the Monbijou Bridge. It was built by Ernst Eberhard von Inhe from 1897 to 1904 and its neo-Baroque design, with a distinctive dome, breaks the Classical convention set by the other buildings on the island. Though all the collections are depleted, the museum is still worth a look. The interior is spectacular, with sweeping staircases, balustrades and marble colonnaded halls.

On the ground floor are stone sculptures (Skulpturensammlung) – mainly damaged statues salvaged from the ruins of various Berlin buildings at the end of World War II. There are also medieval wooden sculptures, notably by 15th-century sculptor Tilman Riemenschneider.

The Far East collection (Fernostsammlung) has art from China, Japan and Korea. The Egyptian collection (Ägyptische Sammlung), though inferior to its twin in Charlottenburg, has an interesting collection of mummies, sarcophagi and statues, though the presentation is rather old-fashioned.

On the first floor are collections of coins (Münzkabinett), early Christian and Byzantine art (Frühchristliche-byzantische Sammlung), including a 6th-century mosaic fragment of Christ and the saints from the church of San Michele in Ravenna, and the picture gallery (Gemäldegalerie), comprising minor German and Flemish works.

Mitte, Monbijou Brücke.
Tel: (030) 209 05577.
www.smb.spk-berlin.de.
Open: Tue–Sun 10am–6pm (Thur 10am–10pm). S-Bahn to Hackescher Markt. Buses: 100 or 200. Trams: 1 & 2.

Galerie der Romantik (Gallery of Romantic Art)

Choice works of the German Romantic school are presented in the gallery, housed in the Alte Nationalgalerie since 2001. Pride of place belongs to Caspar David Friedrich (1774–1840), whose work epitomises the Romantic preoccupation with man's relationship to nature.

Karl Friedrich Schinkel (1781–1841) (*see pp44–5*) made his reputation as an architect, but his talents were by no means confined to building. Schinkel's interest in the medieval world, a typically Romantic passion, is perfectly illustrated by a series of paintings of imaginary Gothic cathedrals set against dramatic natural backdrops.

Less elevated, but of considerable historical interest, are the topographical paintings by Eduard Gärtner, including a mid-19th-century view of Unter den Linden and a study of the Bauakademie, one of Schinkel's finest architectural achievements, bulldozed by the East German authorities in the 1960s. The nearby Schinkel Pavilion, an adjunct to the Gallery, has survived as a testament to the architect's mastery of form.

Displayed in a charming procession of rooms are more paintings from the Romantic period, including a remarkable panorama of the Berlin skyline by Gärtner, from the vantage point of Friedrichswerdersche Kirche.

Mitte. Alte Nationalgalerie/ Museumsinsel. U-Bahn or S-Bahn to Friedrichstrasse. S-Bahn to Hackescher Markt. Buses: 100, 157, 200, 348 to Lustgarten & 147 to Universitätsstrasse. Trams: 1, 2, 3, 4, 5, 6, 50 & 53.

Museum für Islamische Kunst (Museum of Islamic Art)

Housed in the Pergamon Museum, this is a remarkable collection of illuminated Korans and manuscripts, glassware, textiles and ceramics covering the entire Islamic world, from Spain to India. There is also a display of exquisite Ottoman carpets, mainly dating from the 16th and 17th centuries.

Mitte, Am Kupfergraben. Entrance: Pergamonmuseum. www.smb.spk-berlin.de. Open: Tue–Sun 10am–6pm (Thur 10am–10pm). U-Bahn or S-Bahn to Friedrichstrasse. S-Bahn to Hackescher Markt. Buses: 100, 157, 200, 348 to Lustgarten & 147 to Universitätsstrasse. Trams: 1, 2, 3, 4, 5, 6, 50 & 53.

Neues Museum

This neoclassical building, dating from 1843 to 1855, was designed by August Stüler for the Egyptian collection. His original idea, that the wall paintings and décor should harmonise with the contents of the rooms to create a whole work of art, turned out to be impractical. The museum is closed for restoration until early 2009.

Pergamonmuseum (Pergamon Museum)

A marvellous survey of the art and architecture of the ancient world, from Babylon through Sumeria, Assyria and Mesopotamia to classical Greece and Rome. In Hall I feast your eyes on the exhibit which gives the museum its name, the Pergamon Altar. Pergamon (Bergama) lies near the western coast of modern Turkey and was once one of the most important centres of the Hellenistic world. Much of the history of Pergamon is shrouded in obscurity, but it is known that in 165 BC it overcame its Galatean enemies after a prolonged war. This victory is commemorated in the frieze of the battle of the gods and the giants, which can be seen around the walls of the hall. The altar was discovered during excavations from 1878 to 1886. Centuries earlier it had been described by the Roman writer Lucius Ampelius as a wonder of the world.

Hall II contains other outstanding pieces of Hellenistic architecture, including a portico from the temple of Athena in Pergamon. Hall III, on the other side of the Altar, contains a reconstruction of the gateway of the market place in Miletus (western Turkey). Built in AD 120 as the gateway to the city's southern market, it was

No visit to Berlin would be complete without a trip to the Pergamon Museum

originally framed by impressive public buildings. In the 6th century AD the Emperor Justinian incorporated the gateway into the city wall. It was destroyed in an earthquake and had to be pieced together fragment by fragment.

Pass through one gateway into another: the Ishtar Gate from Babylon. Nebuchadnezzar II, who commissioned it, predicted rightly that it would be something 'upon which humankind in its entirety will gaze with wonder'. It was built between 604 and 562 BC and is dedicated to the weather god Adad, whose symbol was the bull, and Marduk, patron of the city, represented by dragons. Ishtar, after whom the gate is named, was the goddess of war – her symbol is the lion.

The processional way, which is also reconstructed in the museum, was originally 20m (66ft) wide and 250m (820ft) long, and played an important part in religious ceremonies. Rooms leading off the processional way exhibit stone vases and animal figurines from Sumeria, a sceptre from Babylon, cuneiform tablets from Assyria, glazed stone reliefs from Persia, and artefacts from excavations at Megiddo and Jericho. A wonderful collection of Greek and Roman statues can be approached from Hall II. The most precious are the Greek originals, including an incomplete mask from Marathon (dating from 470 BC) and a terracotta figure of a Boeotian woman with sunhat and fan which still shows traces of the original gold, red and blue paint.

The highlight of the Department of Islamic Art on the upper floor is a segment of the wall of the palace of Mshatta, a desert fortress of the Caliphs of the 8th-century Umayyad dynasty.
Am Kupfergraben 5.
Tel: (030) 209 05577. www.smb.spk-berlin.de. Open: 10am–6pm (only main rooms on Mon–Tue). Admission charge. U-Bahn or S-Bahn to Friedrichstrasse. S-Bahn to Hackescher Markt.

Neue Synagoge (New Synagogue)

Standing in the heart of the old Jewish quarter, this remarkable building, easily identified by its gleaming onion domes, may once again become the focus of Jewish community life. It was built by two distinguished architects, neither of them Jews, Eduard Knoblauch and August Stüler, and opened in 1866 in the presence of Kaiser William I and his

The onion dome of the Neue Synagoge is a gleaming landmark

prime minister, Otto von Bismarck. The synagogue is large (there is room for 3,200 worshippers), and its design is unashamedly exotic and eclectic – a heady brew of Moorish and Byzantine influences executed in yellow brick. Listed building status protected the synagogue from the worst excesses of the Nazi's 'night of broken glass' (*Reichskristallnacht*), 9 November 1938, when almost all other Jewish monuments and places of worship were destroyed. Ironically, Allied bombs finally devastated the building, which was at the time being used as an ammunition store. A plaque on the wall of the reconstructed synagogue admonishes visitors: 'never forget'. Since 1995, it has functioned again as a place of worship and a centre for Jewish studies (*Centrum Judaicum*). But it is a sad reflection of the times that a policeman guards the entrance.

Nearby, in Grosse Hamburger Strasse, is the site of the **Old Jewish Cemetery**, dating from 1672, when immigrants began arriving from Vienna. Although the cemetery was no longer in use by the time the Nazis came to power, it was desecrated and then destroyed by the Gestapo in 1943.
Oranienburger Strasse 28–30. U-Bahn to Friedrichstrasse or S-Bahn to Oranienburger Strasse.

Neue Wache (New Guardhouse)

The former royal guardhouse (the Palace once stood opposite) was built to a classical design by Schinkel in 1818 to complement the Baroque Zeughaus or Arsenal (now the German Historical Museum), which stands next to it. The ceremony of the changing of the guard began here in the 19th century. After World War I the guardhouse became a monument to Germany's unknown soldier and, after World War II, a 'Memorial to the Victims of Fascism and Militarism'. However, the irony of goose-stepping East German soldiers carrying out their ceremonial duties here was not lost on Berliners, who referred to them as 'Red Prussians'. The soldiers disappeared with the army in which they served in 1990.
Unter den Linden.

Nikolaikirche (St Nicholas Church)

This is Berlin's oldest parish church. A Romanesque basilica stood on the site until 1230, when work on the present building commenced. The Gothic choir and nave were completed in 1470; in 1877 Hermann Blankenstein replaced the tower with two thrusting spires. It was here that the hitherto separate communities of Berlin and Cölln agreed to join in 1307; here, too, that Protestantism was welcomed by Bishop Buchholzer in 1539, a little more than 20 years after Luther's first adversary – the Dominican monk Johannes Tetzel – had preached the need for Catholic reform from the same pulpit. The church is now a museum of the early history of Berlin.
Mitte, Nikolaikirchplatz.
Tel: (030) 240 02182. Open: Tue–Sun

10am–6pm. Closed: 4pm if concert on. Admission charge. U-Bahn or S-Bahn to Alexanderplatz.

Olympiastadion (Olympic Stadium)

Built for the 1936 Summer Olympics, the 76,000-seat stadium remains an exemplar of Third Reich architectural grandiosity (*see map, pp32–3*). It is now 'home field' to the Berlin Hertha BSC football club, and hosted the final match of 2006's World Cup championships.
Spandau, Olympischer Platz 3.
Tel: (030) 250 02322. Open: Wed & Sun 10am–6pm. Admission charge for tours and exhibition. U-Bahn to Olympia-Stadion (east entrance) or S-Bahn to Olympiastadion.

Otto-Nagel-Haus

An exhibition of the work of noted German Expressionist artists such as Otto Nagel (1894–1967), Käthe Kollwitz and Otto Dix.
Mitte, Märkisches Ufer 16. Tel: (030) 279 1424. Open: Wed–Sun 9am–5pm. Admission charge. U-Bahn to Märkisches Museum.

Potsdamer Platz

This place was once Berlin's hotspot, bounded by hotels, restaurants and nightclubs. Allied bombing erased it from the map and the place became wasteland between the East and West for decades. In 1993, Daimler-Benz was the first to reclaim the area with its building, followed by Sony and other investors. The neo-Baroque *Kaisersaal* salons inside the Grand Hotel Esplanade, the outer walls of which have been carefully preserved, form the historic centrepiece of the modern Sony Center, which represents an architectural masterpiece. The Film Museum housing the Marlene Dietrich Collection was opened in September 2000. Sketches, scenery designs, models and countless exhibits document developments in German film from 1919 to the present. New cafés and restaurants, a shopping mall, casino, cinemas and a musical theatre now welcome life again in the place where Berlin danced in the Golden Twenties.
S-Bahn or U-Bahn to Potsdamer Platz.

Reichstag (Parliament)

One of Berlin's most distinctive landmarks and a potent symbol of its troubled history, the parliament building gained a new lease of life

Parliament past and present – the Reichstag building with the new dome

Berlin's Town Hall is the symbol of a newly unified community

following the decision in June 1991 to move the German seat of government back to Berlin from Bonn. The Reichstag was designed by Paul Wallot in 1884 and completed ten years later; its shallow dome had to be dismantled for safety after World War II.

Although an inscription on one of the external walls dedicates it to the German people, the Reichstag's associations with democratic government are ambiguous, to say the least. Before World War I it was effectively the Prussian aristocracy, not parliament, that ruled Germany. In November 1918 the republic was proclaimed from the Reichstag, but little more than a year later conditions verging on civil war forced the new national assembly to meet in the small provincial town of Weimar. In February 1933 the Nazis used the excuse of the Reichstag being set on fire to do away with parliament altogether.

The building was even further damaged at the end of the war, when the Soviets entered Berlin. The central dome was removed during the reconstruction. After reunification the decision was made to move the Bundestag from Bonn back to Berlin and to revitalise the Reichstag. The reconstruction started in 1995 and was completed in 1999. Sir Norman Foster's design added a glass dome over the plenary hall, which has become a major attraction for tourists. Since April 1999, the Reichstag has once again become the seat of the National Parliament. You can visit the building and walk all the way to the top of the dome. Allow for waiting times of one hour or more.
Tiergarten, Platz der Republik.
Tel: (030) 22732 152. Open: Tue–Sun 10am–5pm. Free admission. S-Bahn to Unter den Linden. Buses: 100 & 123.

Rotes Rathaus (Red Town Hall)

Named for the colour of the brick, not the politics of the city fathers, the 104m- (341ft-) high tower is an unmistakable landmark for Berlin's

residents. It was completed in 1869 from a design by Heinrich Friedrich Waesemann and is loosely modelled on the Renaissance town halls of northern Italy. When the city was divided, the Rotes Rathaus appropriately became the municipal headquarters of East Berlin, while the West adopted Rathaus Schöneberg. The Rotes Rathaus now serves both communities. A frieze installed at the building's east entrance commemorates the city's 'rubble women' (*Trümmerfrauen*), who worked tirelessly at clearing and salvaging bomb-blasted Berlin's enormous piles of debris immediately following the cessation of World War II hostilities.
Alexanderplatz/Spandauer Strasse. S-Bahn to Alexanderplatz.

Rykestrasse Synagoge

Ornate neo-Romanesque house of Jewish worship dating from 1904, abandoned during Nazi-era repressions, restored and reopened in 2007. Now Germany's largest working synagogue, with seating capacity for 1,074 people.
Prenzlauer Berg, Rykestrasse. Open for tours: Thur 2–6pm (4pm in English). Free admission. U-Bahn to Senefelder Platz.

Sachsenhausen

See pp110–11.

St-Hedwigs-Kathedrale

Berlin's Roman Catholic cathedral was inspired by the Roman Pantheon (the interior does bear a passing resemblance) – or was it an upturned coffee cup which influenced Frederick the Great's choice of design? The church was built between 1747 and 1773 by Knobelsdorff and Johann Boumann, but the outsize green dome, which distracts from the fine pediment and massive Ionic columns, was not completed until the end of the 19th century. For a long time this was the only Catholic place of worship in this overwhelmingly Protestant city.
Mitte, Bebelplatz. Tel: (030) 203 4810. Open: Mon–Sat 10am–5pm, Sun 1–5pm. Free admission. U-Bahn to Hausvogteiplatz. Buses: 100, 147, 157, 257 & 348.

Scheunenviertel

Lying just to the north of Museum Island and Monbijou Park, the 'barn quarter' of Berlin was where Jewish migrants settled in the 1670s after the Great Elector Frederick William offered them a safe haven from persecution in Austria. (The gesture was not an altruistic one – the refugees were expected to bring their considerable wealth with them.) During the relatively tolerant 18th century, the community thrived and, through distinguished leaders such as Moses Mendelssohn, made an important contribution to the commercial and cultural life of the city. By 1850 the wealthier families were moving into more salubrious parts of the city, while the Scheunenviertel deteriorated into the slum that Theodore Fontane described in his novels. Despite this, tradition determined that the prestigious New Synagogue was built here in the 1860s (*see pp78–9*).

By 1910 Jews were as well represented in Berlin as the Turks are today. It was this prominence, coupled with envy at the distinction they had achieved in every walk of life from journalism and publishing to science and banking, that brought them to the attention of racist ideologues. When the Nazis came to power in 1933 the party's propaganda chief, Joseph Goebbels, made a particular point of equating the appalling living conditions and criminal reputation of the Scheunenviertel with the Jewish presence.

The New Synagogue, though not severely damaged, was attacked on *Reichskristallnacht* (9 November 1938), after which the fate of the Jews was sealed. From 1942, more than 55,000 Berlin Jews were taken to an old people's home on Grosse Hamburger Strasse before being transported to Auschwitz and other extermination camps. (A monument to the victims of fascism stands on the site.) Today, there are only 5,000 Jews in Berlin but the synagogue survives, as does the site of the Old Jewish Cemetery (*see p79*). The heart of this interesting quarter, Oranienburger Strasse, is still rather run-down but there is an undercurrent of 1960s radical chic.
S-Bahn to Hackescher Markt.

Schloss Babelsberg

King Frederick William III commissioned Karl Friedrich Schinkel to design a summer residence for his family in 1833. At the request of his wife, it was modelled on Britain's Windsor Castle, which the couple

Royal retreat – neo-Gothic Schloss Babelsberg, modelled on Windsor Castle

had visited a few years earlier. The neo-Gothic Schloss was subsequently enlarged to accommodate a greater number of guests. The fabulous park, with views across the Havel towards Potsdam, Schloss Glienicke and the Glienicke Bridge, was laid out by Peter Joseph Lenné and Hermann Puckler-Muskau in 1833–5. Perched on the water's edge is the Kleines Schloss (Small Castle), built in 1841 for Princess Augusta's ladies-in-waiting. Schloss Babelsberg was a favourite with the King for the remainder of his life. Most of the leading politicians of the day attended him here at some time or other, including the 'Iron Chancellor', Bismarck, on the occasion of his appointment as Minister President of Prussia in 1862 – an event with profound consequences for the future of Germany.

Potsdam, Auf dem Babelsberg.
Tel: (0331) 969 4250. Admission charge.
Buses: 116 or 216 to Schloss Glienicke, then walk or take bus 691.

Schöneberg district

The medieval village of Sconenberch received its charter in 1264 and remained independent from Berlin until 1920. By that time it was already a desirable residential suburb, thanks to the land speculators who moved in after the Wars of Unification. By the 1920s the character of Schöneberg had changed. The area around Nollendorfplatz had become a centre of gay life, as the English novelist Christopher Isherwood famously

The Liberty Bell in Schöneberg town hall, where President Kennedy made his famous speech

testifies in his Berlin novels, *Mr Norris Changes Trains* and *Goodbye to Berlin* (on which the film *Cabaret* is based). Isherwood himself lived 'the life of the unemployed' at 17 Nollendorfstrasse from March 1929 until February 1933, and paints an unflattering picture.

When the Nazis came to power, the character of the area changed once again. The nightclubs were closed down, homosexuals and other 'deviants' persecuted, and the Sportspalast on Pallas Strasse (no longer standing) became one of Hitler's favourite venues for speechmaking.

Schöneberg's town hall (Rathaus Schöneberg), on Martin-Luther-Strasse, was home to West Berlin's municipal government from 1948 to 1989, and it was from this balcony that US President John F Kennedy made his famous '*Ich bin ein Berliner*' speech before half a million people on 26 June 1963.

U-Bahn to Nollendorfplatz.

Schwules Museum (Gay Museum)

One of the best museums in the world dedicated to gay themes, this successfully draws together the whole fabric of homosexual life. There is a museum, library, archive and photographs to tell you everything you could ever want to know on gay issues, lifestyle, culture and politics.

Kreuzberg, Mehringdamm 61. Tel: (030) 693 1172. Open: Wed–Mon 2–6pm (Sat 2–7pm). Admission charge. U-Bahn to Mehringdamm.

Siegessäule (Victory Column)

The location of this monument on Grosser Stern, a radial point of five avenues surrounded by the Tiergarten, seems so ideal that it comes as a surprise to learn that it was moved here by Hitler in 1938 from its original position on the square in front of the Reichstag. He intended it to be the focal point of Nazi parades along the Strasse des 17 Juni, then known as the East–West Axis.

The Victory Column was erected in 1873 to commemorate Prussian success in the Wars of Unification against, successively, Denmark, Austria and France. Reliefs showing military exploits of the era decorate the inner walls, and the fluted sandstone column, 69m (227ft) high and built on a colonnaded pedestal of red granite, is ornamented with captured cannons. The oversized statue of Victory which crowns the summit weighs 35 tonnes and is known to Berliners as 'Gold Else'.

The Victory Column

Approach the entrance from the subway on Strasse des 17 Juni and it is possible to climb the 285 steps to the viewing platform, with splendid views across the Tiergarten towards the Reichstag and the Brandenburg Gate – ideal for photographs.

Tiergarten, Grosser Stern. Tel: (030) 391 2961. Open: Mon 1–6pm, Tue–Sun 9am–5.30pm. Admission charge. U-Bahn to Hansaplatz. S-Bahn to Bellevue. Bus: 100 to Grosser Stern.

Skulpturensammlung und Museum für Byzanthinische Kunst (Sculpture Collection and Museum of Byzantine Art)

This is a breathtaking collection of sculptures from the late classical period to the 19th century and includes icons

(*Cont. on p88*)

Berlin evolution

'Berlin is always becoming, never being,' said the art critic Karl Scheffler in 1910. The city is never content with standing still. Towards the end of the 1990s, Germany's old-new capital was labelled Europe's biggest building site, with construction cranes looming and swivelling on the spread-out urban skyline. Since then, the projects have settled into a strong semblance of completeness and cohesiveness.

By the early years of the 21st century, a strikingly futuristic government district stands proudly by the River Spree. Nearby, construction of the city's main railway station gives the travelling public a skylit, multi-level facility. From there, a short southward walk brings you to the Reichstag – steeped in turbulent history, where parliamentary Bundestag votes are cast once again – topped dramatically by its new glass dome (*see pp80–81*). Turn from there, by way of Tiergarten greenery, to reach resurrected Potsdamer Platz (*see pp80 & 103*), the best-known of all 1990s mega-developments, which reconnects Western and Eastern Berlin quite effectively.

The city's regained worldliness has several aspects; for instance, a batch of newly built embassies in the Pariser Platz/Brandenburg Gate vicinity and a greatly expanded gateway airport, Berlin Brandenburg International,

The face of Berlin is constantly changing, with futuristic construction such as the gleaming Sony Center replacing the now redundant monuments to Communism

which will replace outdated, rather forlorn Schönefeld Flughafen upon completion three years hence. Another changeover has affected Reichsmarschall Hermann Göring's Luftwaffe Air Ministry, built in 1934–6, on Leipzigerstrasse. That mammoth showpiece of ego was transformed into the Federal Ministry of Finance in 1994. And forget about finding Hitler's bunker; it is now buried deep beneath bland rows of apartment blocks.

Commercial redevelopment is a priority in the East. The massive 1995 complex at Friedrichstadt-Passagen contains shops with restaurants, offices, apartments and galleries. To encourage visitors to stray east from the Brandenburg Gate, a new underground line has been built to link the Ku'damm with Friedrichstrasse and Alexanderplatz. Berliners take a keen interest in the future of their city, and many of the proposed projects have aroused fierce controversy. One example was Daimler-Benz's acquistion of sections of Potsdamer Platz for high-rise offices before alternative proposals to recreate the carefree atmosphere of pre-war days could be considered.

Greater sensitivity has been shown in deciding the future of Berlin Mitte's Lustgarten area. In summertime 1993, a highly entertaining and imaginative exhibition became the vehicle for debating whether to rebuild Schlüter's masterpiece, the Hohenzollern rulers' Schloss. In July 2002, the decision was finally made to reconstruct the baroque behemoth. The asbestos-plagued Palast der Republic, which has occupied the site since 1976, is expected to be pulled down by late 2008 despite protests by those who want to keep the grotesque Socialist showpiece as part of the GDR's history.

The ceiling 'sails' of the new Sony Center change colour throughout the evening

Berlin has always had a problem with identity. 'Berlin is a great city, a world city (perhaps?)' wrote Kaiser William II before World War II. Looking to the future, the new tourism officials have declared their intention to remove the query and make Berlin undeniably a world city, on a par with London, Paris, Rome and New York.

and mosaics, medieval religious statuary, and some fine examples from the Renaissance and Baroque periods. The sculpture gallery, which began under the Great Elector (1640–88), now contains some 1,200 works of sculpture and is divided into five sections: Early Christian and Byzantine, medieval sculpture, the Italian collection, Renaissance and Baroque sculpture from north of the Alps, and sculpture of the 19th century.

The Byzantine era is represented by icons, mosaics and ivories, including a diptych dating from the middle of the 6th century. The medieval collection is astonishingly rich, given the iconoclasm which led to the destruction of so many religious objects during the Reformation in Europe. Among the earliest examples is a dignified figure of Mary, mourning the loss of her son (*c.*1230). Also look out for a serene Christ and St John, from Lake Constance (*c.*1320), and another graceful carving of Mary, from Lindenholz (1480), which depicts the Mother of God as a golden-robed beauty protecting a group of medieval worshippers in the folds of her blue mantle. *The Palm Sunday Christ on a Donkey* from Landshut would originally have been pulled along in the Holy Week procession – hence the platform on wheels. The donkey and platform are modern replacements but the figure of Christ is original (*c.*1200). Especially absorbing is *The Calvary*, commissioned in about 1490 by the famous Augsburg banking family of Fugger, with over 30 figures gathered at the scene of the Crucifixion.

The upper floor begins with a room devoted to the work of Tilman Riemenschneider and includes his wrought carvings of the four evangelists, each individually characterised. The Italian collection includes a marble relief by Donatello, and sculptures by Bernini and Giovanni Bologna.

Mitte, Am Kupfergraben. Entrance: Bode Museum: Monbijou Brücke. U-Bahn or S-Bahn to Friedrichstrasse. S-Bahn to Hackescher Markt. Buses: 100, 157, 200, 348 to Lustgarten & 147 to Universitätsstrasse. Trams: 1, 2, 3, 4, 5, 6, 50 & 53.

Spandau district

Situated about 12km (7$^1/_2$ miles) northwest of Berlin centre, Spandau, founded in 1232, is the city's oldest suburb. Its site, at the confluence of the rivers Havel and Spree, made it an ideal trading post and an important strategic point, which is why Spandau has had a castle since the 13th century. In more recent times, Spandau was famous as the place of incarceration of Hitler's deputy, Rudolf Hess. Hess was sentenced to life imprisonment by the Nuremberg Tribunal and served a total of 41 years, more than 20 of them as the gaol's sole prisoner. Despite a public outcry, the Soviet government refused to release him and he committed suicide in 1987 at the age of 93. (While Spandau itself was in the Western sector, the gaol was administered jointly by all four Allied powers, including the Soviet Union.) The prison was immediately flattened and the site became a supermarket for the British forces stationed there.

The **Zitadelle** (Citadel), like the old town itself, is situated on an island, and its red-brick fortifications, surrounded by a moat, are unmistakable. The crenellated Julius Tower is the oldest surviving part of the building and dates from about 1200; the core of the remainder is Renaissance, designed by an Italian architect for the Elector Joachim II of Brandenburg in 1557. Inside the cobbled courtyard is a statue of Berlin's founder, Albert the Bear. Immediately to his right are the ruins of the old arsenal, destroyed by Napoleon in 1813. The Old Magazine dates from 1580 but the bastions and the new arsenal are 19th century. Cannon were manufactured in a foundry near Spandau in the 1850s. In 1860 a brand-new model was sent on an 11,000km (6,835-mile) journey to the Russian settlement of Khabarovsk in the Far East. It languished there for more than a century but has eventually been returned, the journey paid for by local businessmen.

Zitadelle *Strasse am Juliusturm 1/20. Open: Tue–Fri 9am–5pm, Sat–Sun 10am–5pm. Admission charge. U-Bahn to Zitadelle Bahnhof.*
Gotisches Haus *Breite Strasse 32. Open: Tue–Fri 10am–5pm, Sat–Sun 10am–1pm. Free admission.*

Despite wartime bombing, the half-timbered houses and cottages of the Altstadt (Old Town) have been well preserved. The **Gotisches Haus** at

Spandau's island citadel, reminder of an independent past

Breite Strasse 32 is Berlin's oldest building, now the town museum. Outside the sturdy, 15th-century Nikolaikirche in Reformationsplatz is a monument to the Reformation, erected in 1889 to commemorate the introduction of Protestantism to Mark Brandenburg. The picturesque area to the northeast, known as the Kolk, boasts a lock, quaint old houses and remains of the town wall.
U-Bahn to Altstadt-Spandau.

Stasi Museum

Spying was big business and a many-tentacled monster in the days of the GDR. Operations were masterminded from the Ministerium für Staatssicherheit (Stasi) headquarters, which is now a museum (*see map, pp32–3*). Alongside busts of Marx and Lenin, the museum houses relics of Cold War spying operations including hidden spy cameras. You can enter the office of former secret police chief Erich Mielke.
Ministerium für Staatssicherheit Forschungs- und Gedenkstätte Normannenstrasse. Lichtenberg, Ruschestr-103. Tel: (030) 553 6854. www.stasimuseum.de. Open: Mon–Fri 11am–6pm, Sat–Sun 2–6pm.

The Stasi Museum in the old headquarters of the East German secret police

Admission charge. Guided tours available (book in advance). U-Bahn to Magdalenstrasse.

Story of Berlin

This multimedia experience delves into the daily lives of Berliners through 800-plus years of their urban existence, involvements, challenges and World War II dangers. Downstairs from the exhibit halls, visitors have access to a 1970s nuclear fallout bunker that was roomy enough to accommodate 3,500 citizens during Cold War tensions.
Charlottenburg, Kurfürstendamm 207–208. Tel: (030) 887 20100. Open: daily 10am–8pm. Admission charge. U-Bahn to Uhlandstrasse or Kurfürstendamm. S-Bahn to Savignyplatz.

Tempelhof

Nowadays Tempelhof is a conventional civilian airport carrying passengers to and from various destinations in Germany and Western Europe, but it still has a distinctive atmosphere. There are no motorway approaches because it is in the heart of the city. There are hardly any signposts, and the terminal itself is hidden from view.

In 1948, at the height of the Cold War, things were very different. On 23 June the Soviet authorities abruptly announced that all road and rail routes to and from West Berlin were closed 'because of technical problems'. This disingenuous message signalled the start of an 11-month blockade, an attempt to starve the population of West Berlin into surrender, and to force the Allies out of the city. The first instinct of the US military governor, General Lucius Clay, was to prise open the land route by confronting the Communists head-on, but it was eventually decided to supply the beleaguered citizens by air, using the US Tempelhof airbase, British-sector Gatow and French-sector Tegel airfields.

From 26 June 1948 to 12 May 1949 US Dakota C-47 transport planes and specially converted British Lancasters and flying boats made a total of 300,000 flights and managed to drop more than 1.8 million tonnes of supplies – food, fuel and medicine – over the western zones of the city. More than 70 lives were lost, but the Soviets surrendered and the blockade was lifted. A memorial outside the airport commemorates the event.
U-Bahn to Platz der Luftbrücke.

Topographie des Terrors

A large prefabricated hut stands on the site of the School of Industrial Arts and Crafts; from May 1933 this was the headquarters of the Gestapo (State Secret Police) and Prinz-Albrecht-Strasse 8 soon became 'the most feared address in Berlin'. Those arrested were driven through the twin brick pillars of the garden gate (still standing) and into the basement to await interrogation and torture. The flattened-out area beneath a canopy to the side of the hut marks the site of the cell block where prisoners were held for months, sometimes years, before being moved on to the larger gaols and concentration camps of the Third Reich. The SS also owned the next-door building (formerly a hotel) and the imposing Prinz-Albrecht Palais which fronted on to Wilhelmstrasse. In these premises the worst of the war crimes perpetrated by the Nazi regime were conceived, organised and overseen by Heinrich Himmler's evil legionaries, including Reinhard Heydrich, Ernst Kaltenbrunner and Adolf Eichmann.

The exhibition hall is built over the foundations of an annexe to Gestapo headquarters, containing a kitchen and canteen built by prisoners from Sachsenhausen concentration camp between 1943 and 1944. Inside is photographic documentation charting the history of the buildings which once occupied the site, the rise and expansion of the Nazi state, the consequences of its racist and expansionist policies, the fate of its opponents and the careers of its leading executives.

Outside, a wooden flight of steps leads to a viewing platform which looks out over the area, known during the War as the Regierungsviertel (Government Quarter). The future of the site is still a subject of controversy. There are those who believe it is time to bury the past and use this prime site for urban redevelopment. Others argue that the darker pages of Germany's past must be confronted, and it was this view that prompted the organisation of the Topographie des Terrors exhibition in 1987 (Berlin's 750th anniversary). Plans for a more permanent memorial have still to be finalised.

Kreuzberg, Niederkirchnerstrasse 8. Tel: (030) 25486 703. www.topographie.de. Open: daily 10am–6pm. Free admission. U-Bahn or S-Bahn to Anhalter Bahnhof. U-Bahn to Kochstrasse.

Unter den Linden

This 1.6km (1-mile) long avenue (*see pp98–9*), running from the Brandenburg Gate to Museumsinsel, became the incongruous heart of East Berlin when the city was divided after World War II. Incongruous, because Unter den Linden ('Under the Limes') had been the symbol of Prussian imperialism for hundreds of years, and had become, during the 18th and 19th centuries, the setting for a string of grandiose neoclassical buildings, including cathedrals, palaces, museums and embassies.

Originally a route for royal hunting parties heading for the Tiergarten woods, Unter den Linden was laid out in 1648 by Elector Frederick William, who had the first lime trees planted along its length. The avenue's role as an imperial showpiece was developed in the 18th century, with the erection of the Deutsche Staatsoper, St-Hedwigs-Kathedrale (*see p82*), both designed by Knobelsdorff for Frederick the Great, and the Alte Königliche Bibliothek

(Old Royal Library), all of which were set around a square known as the Forum Fridericianum, now called Bebelplatz (*see pp98–9*). The theme of imperial pomp was continued in the 19th and early 20th centuries with the addition of Schinkel's Neue Wache, the palace guardhouse, built in 1818 to resemble a Roman temple (*see p79*), and the Protestant Cathedral, the Berliner Dom, which opened in 1905 at the lower end of the avenue (*see p30*).

Communist rule brought many changes to Unter den Linden, already ravaged by Allied air raids. The Kaiser's palace was demolished and eventually replaced with Erich Honecker's modern Palast der Republik in 1976; the equestrian statue of Frederick the Great, removed from its site outside the Humboldt University in 1950, was returned in the 1980s; modern blocks were hurriedly built to fill bomb sites; names of streets and functions of buildings were changed. Monuments were raised to victims of Fascism and the lime trees that had been cut down by Hitler to make room for Nazi processions were replanted.

With the Berlin Wall gone, Unter den Linden has now resumed its role as a focus for a unified city; as such, its future development is sure to reflect the new aspirations and problems of Berlin.

The famous lime trees of Unter den Linden

Walk: Around Ku'damm

This walk explores Berlin's exciting West End and its shopping centre.

Allow about 1 to 1½ hours.

Start at Bahnhof Zoologischer Garten. Leave the station by the Hardenbergplatz exit.

1 Bahnhof Zoologischer Garten

After dark, Bahnhof Zoo is the haunt of the city's youth on the way to a night out; by day it's a busy transit point for commuters and backpackers. Once you arrive here you know you are in the heart of modern Berlin: the excitement is infectious, the pace frenetic. Across the road is the neo-Romanesque Kaiser Wilhelm Gedächtniskirche (Memorial Church – *see p60*) and Breitscheidplatz, where anything goes, from busking and fund-raising stunts to street fairs and rock concerts.

Cross over into Joachimstaler Strasse, pass the Kaiser Wilhelm Gedächtniskirche (Memorial Church), and turn left into Tauentzienstrasse. Continue past the Europa-Center and the KaDeWe department store to Wittenbergplatz.

2 Wittenbergplatz

This neoclassical station has a remarkable 1920s Art Deco interior with a large, hangar-like booking hall and wooden ticket office. Most striking, however, are the colourful period posters advertising Opel cars, the German Automobile Club, Bechstein pianos, Café Möhring and the city's electric tramways.

Return along the same route to Kurfürstendamm.

3 Kurfürstendamm

Flushed with victory over the French in 1871, the Chancellor of the newly united Germany, Otto von Bismarck, planned a grand avenue, on the lines of the Champs Elysées in Paris, to run westwards from the Tiergarten. The building boom which followed led speculators to develop a new West End, encompassing the former villages of Schöneberg, Wilmersdorf and Charlottenburg. These suburbs became the nest of the *nouveaux riches* and of the professional classes. Not long afterwards, the Ku'damm began to rival Friedrichstrasse as a centre of Berlin nightlife.

Following World War II, US investment, dictated by the exigencies of the Cold War, led to the rebuilding of the devastated avenue as a capitalist showcase and a goad to East Berlin. Although it has lost some of its gloss, even today the Ku'damm remains a paradise for shoppers, with wide, tree-shrouded pavements, a diverting café scene, colourful streetlife and plenty of public transport.

Turn left into Fasanenstrasse.

4 Fasanenstrasse

The handsome mansions in this street date from the 1890s. Of particular interest is No 23, the **Literaturhaus**, which has a bookshop in the basement (Kohlhaas und Co), a cultural centre, and an art gallery with a delightful garden café, the Wintergarten. Next door is the **Käthe-Kollwitz-Museum** (*see p61*). At No 25 is another *Jugendstil* villa, the **Villa Grisebach**, built between 1891 and 1895 by Hans Grisebach, and now a private art gallery.

At Fasanenplatz, turn right into Ludwigkirchstrasse.

5 Ludwigkirchplatz

Pleasantly secluded gardens, in front of the church, make an ideal place for resting the feet and sorting out one's impressions. A quietly splashing fountain calms frayed nerves and there is a playground to divert the youngsters.

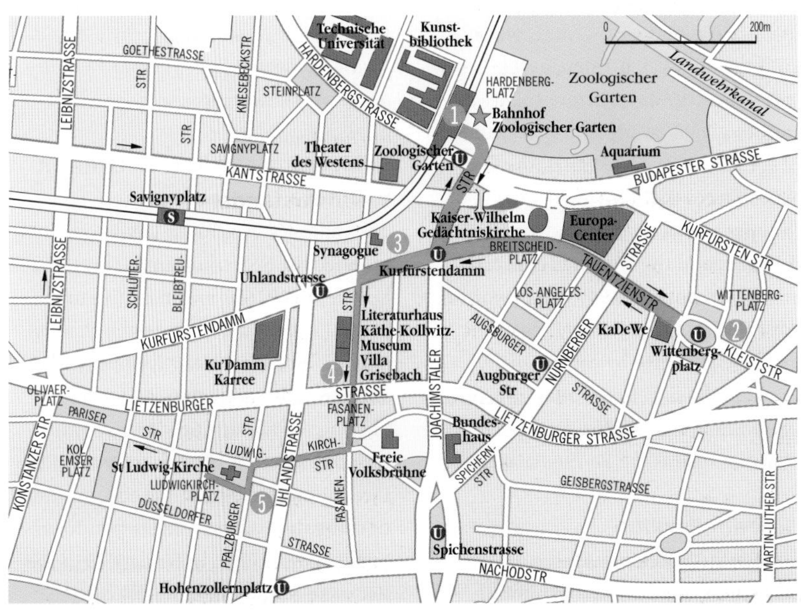

Walk: Tiergarten

This walk takes you through Berlin's most famous park and away from the rush and bustle of the city.

Allow 2 hours.

Begin from Tiergarten S-Bahn station.

1 Tiergarten

Literally the Animal Garden, this park was once a royal forest stocked with wild boar and deer for the hunt. In 1745 Frederick the Great commissioned G N Knobelsdorff to enhance the land with statues and paths, but it was not until the 1830s that Peter Joseph Lenné redesigned the 212-hectare (524-acre) park to give it its present appearance. At the end of World War II, the few blasted trees that remained were chopped down by cold and starving Berliners and the land was converted into allotments. In 1949 the mayor of West Berlin, Ernst Reuter, began the park's renaissance by ceremonially planting the first tree. Today, it is once again the Berliners' favourite park.

On your right is the Berlin-Pavillon.

2 Berlin-Pavillon

The Berlin-Pavillon houses a permanent architectural exhibition of plans for the future development of Berlin.

Open: Tue–Sun 10am–8pm.

Cross Strasse des 17 Juni and follow the path Grosser Weg. To the right of the pathway is the Karl Liebknecht memorial. Turn right at the end of Grosser Weg into Lichtensteinallee and follow to the canal bridge, where a bronze plaque commemorates Rosa Luxemburg and Karl Liebknecht.

3 Memorials to Karl Liebknecht and Rosa Luxemburg

The radical socialist Karl Liebknecht founded the Spartakusbund (Spartacus League) in 1916 as an alternative to the Social Democratic Party. In the chaotic aftermath of World War I, while workers and revolutionaries engaged in street fighting with returning soldiers, Liebknecht and his Polish comrade, Rosa Luxemburg, were planning a Communist uprising. It was immediately put down by the government. In January 1919 the two were forced out of hiding by the

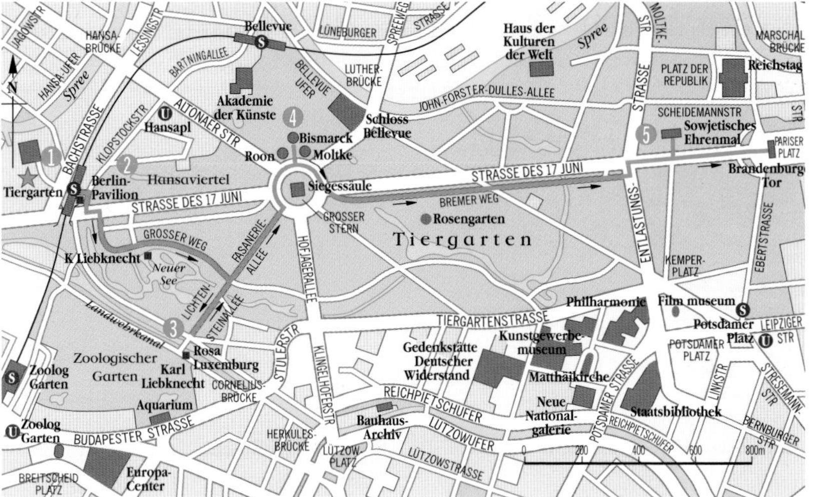

right-wing Free Corps, interrogated, beaten and murdered; their bodies were subsequently discovered in the Landwehrkanal.

Return along Lichtensteinallee and continue along Fasaneriеallee as far as Grosser Stern. Cross the roundabout, passing the Siegessäule (Victory Column). Take the footpath through the trees to the Bismarck monument.

4 Monuments to Bismarck, Moltke and Roon

The three heroes of the Franco-Prussian War – two generals and the future unifier of Germany – are commemorated in statuary of varying degrees of pretension. The Bismarck monument was originally positioned close to the Reichstag and was moved to its present site by Hitler in 1938.

From the Bismarck monument cross Strasse des 17 Juni and take the Bremer Weg. The second path on the right leads through the Rosengarten. Take the path in an easterly direction through the Tiergarten to the Entlastungs-Strasse. Rejoin the Strasse des 17 Juni. On the left is the Soviet memorial.

5 Sowjetisches Ehrenmal

A grandiose monument in Socialist Realist style, using marble from the ruins of Hitler's Chancellery, this memorial commemorates the 20,000 soldiers of the Red Army who perished in the battle for Berlin. The Russian inscription reads: 'Eternal glory to the fallen heroes in battle with the German Fascist aggressor for the freedom and independence of the Soviet Union.' Two Soviet T-34 tanks stand on mute guard at the entrance to the garden.

Pass through the Brandenburger Tor to Pariser Platz.

Walk: Unter den Linden

This stroll takes you through the historic centre of Berlin.

Allow 1½ hours.

Begin at Unter den Linden S-Bahn station.

1 Unter den Linden

At one time this was the heart of Imperial Berlin, where Prussian soldiers paraded, bands played, and crowds promenaded, and where tourists flocked to admire the succession of architectural set pieces which adorned the lower end of the avenue (*see* Berliner Dom, *pp30 & 93*).

By way of contrast, the top end of the avenue remains an unhappy aggregate of building sites, little-patronised modish shops and relics of a bygone era – the offices of Intourist, Aeroflot and the Russian Embassy. The four rows of lime trees from which the avenue takes its name are still here, but its original purpose as a processional route leading from the Schloss to the Brandenburg Gate has been lost.

Continue to Charlottenstrasse. Turn right, cross Französische Strasse, then left into Gendarmenmarkt (see pp54–5).

2 Schauspielhaus (Playhouse/National Theatre)

This fine neoclassical building (*see p55*) by Schinkel was erected between 1818 and 1821. The statues and sculptures decorating its exterior were executed by Rauch and Christian Friedrich Tieck to designs by Schinkel. The auditorium is now a concert hall. Outside the theatre is a towering marble figure of Friedrich Schiller (1759–1805), most famous as the writer of *Ode to Joy*, the text of Beethoven's *Choral Symphony*.

Return to Französische Strasse and turn right, then left into Bebelplatz.

3 Bebelplatz

Formerly Opernplatz, the square now takes its name from August Bebel, leader of the German Social Democratic party before World War I. It was designed as part of the Forum Fredericianum, Frederick the Great's tribute to himself and to the grandeur of Ancient Rome, which he intended Berlin to emulate. The city's first theatre, the neoclassical Deutsche Staatsoper, stands in the centre of the square. Mendelssohn, Liszt, Richard Strauss and the great conductor Wilhelm Furtwängler all gave performances here. On 10 May 1933, the Nazi propaganda chief, Joseph Goebbels, orchestrated a public book-burning in the square, consigning the works of many eminent authors, including Sigmund Freud, Karl Marx and Thomas Mann, to the flames for being 'un-German in spirit'. At the western end of the square is the Universitätsbibliothek (University Library), built from 1775 to 1780 by Georg Unger and known as the *kommode* because of its supposed resemblance to a chest of drawers.

Leave Bebelplatz and cross Unter den Linden to the Zeughaus.

4 Zeughaus (Arsenal)

Now the Deutsches Historisches Museum, this is Berlin's first and arguably most distinguished Baroque palace, designed by Johann Nering in 1695.

Open: Thur–Tue 10am–6pm. Admission charge for temporary exhibitions. Cross over into Oberwallstrasse, then left into Werderstrasse, passing Friedrichs-Werdersche-Kirche. Cross Schleusen Brücke into Lustgarten.

5 Lustgarten

The Royal Palace, the Stadtschloss, once occupied this site; there are now plans to reconstruct it. The adjacent square was the seat of the East German government; you can still see the white former Foreign Ministry and the gigantic Palast der Republik (1973–6), intended as a lasting monument to socialism but now destined for the scrapheap.

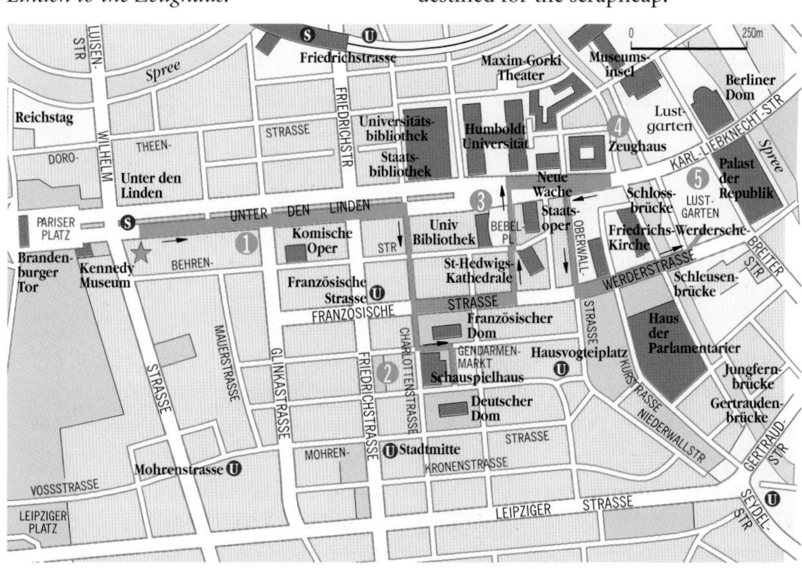

The Berlin Wall

One day in August 1961 the residents of Bernauer Strasse woke up to find armed policemen hastily laying rows of barbed wire immediately outside their front doors. There was no room in this densely built-up neighbourhood of Prenzlauerberg for a wall or even a fence, so the houses themselves became a makeshift barrier between East and West.
As the implications of what was happening began to dawn on the bewildered inhabitants, their first thought was of escape. Leaving by the front door or ground-floor windows quickly became impossible when the authorities ordered all exits facing the street to be bricked up. In desperation, men, women and children began leaping from upper-storey windows. Firemen on the western side tried to break their fall,

A relic of the past, the wall is now a memorial and a tourist attraction but 20 people died, some under a hail of bullets. The remaining residents of Bernauer Strasse were trapped in the East, powerless to do anything except wave forlornly to their loved ones from the tops of their stepladders.

Escape from the bricked-up houses was no longer an option; other ways had to be found. In 1964, more than 30 people made their way to freedom through a tiny, unlit tunnel in the cellar of a bakery. To prevent a recurrence, the authorities demolished much of the street to make way for a fortification 100m (328ft) wide, patrolled by guards and dogs and overlooked by watchtowers. The final symbol of hope – the Church of the Reconciliation – was left stranded in the death strip.

The fate of Bernauer Strasse and its inhabitants finds echoes in the experience of all Berliners, so it is fitting that it was residents of that street who, at 9.15pm on the evening of 9 November 1989, became the first East Berliners to cross freely to the West in more than 28 years. Today, remnants of the wall are clearly visible along the hill that is still called Bernauer Strasse. Here and there a luxuriant overgrowth of weeds and long grass gives way to barren stretches of cinder track, peppered with concrete posts and unwired junction boxes. Wreaths and wooden crosses remind visitors of those who

A section of the wall as it was before demolition

died here, in anticipation of a more permanent memorial to the wall that once cruelly divided a city.

For more information on the history of the Wall and its impact on the people of Berlin, visit the Checkpoint Charlie Museum (*see p58*).

See also the Walk on pp102–3.

WALL STATISTICS

Length 166km (103 miles)
Height 4m (13ft)
295 watchtowers
43 bunkers
262 dog runs
14,000 border guards
80 fatalities, including 25 guards

Walk: The Wall

This walk follows part of the route of the former Berlin Wall.

Allow 3 hours.

Start at Kochstrasse U-Bahn and walk north into Friedrichstrasse.

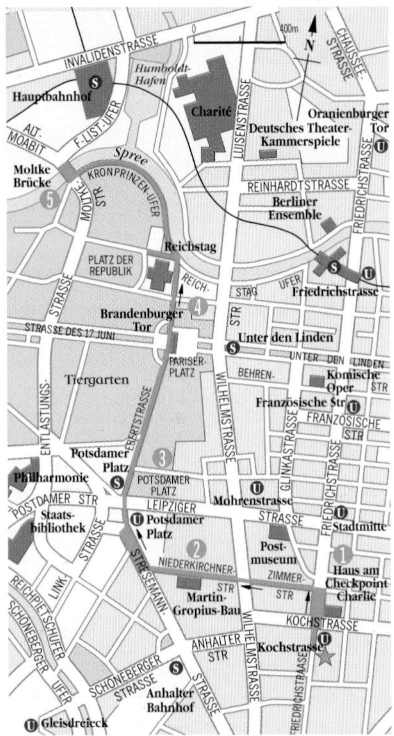

1 Haus am Checkpoint Charlie

Alpha, Bravo, Charlie . . . Of all the border posts only Charlie, located at that most sensitive of spots, the Friedrichstrasse, captured the popular imagination. Here, in October 1961, US and Soviet tanks confronted one another in a dangerous game of 'call my bluff' while the politicians wrangled over the issue of Allied military access to East Berlin. On 22 June 1990, Charlie, now surplus to requirements, was finally hoisted away by crane, to the accompaniment of brass bands and a military parade, the last by the former joint occupying powers.

Turn left into Zimmerstrasse, where you will see a wooden cross marking the grave of 18-year-old Peter Fechter, who bled to death while trying to escape over the Wall in 1962.

2 Niederkirchnerstrasse

It is already becoming difficult to appreciate how formidable the Wall was at the height of its monstrous development. Behind the frontline concrete barrier, covered with smooth piping to make gripping difficult, was the death strip, a 100m- (328ft-) wide zone of ancillary fences, guard-dog tracks, anti-vehicle trenches, alarms and observation towers. Few managed to survive this murderous obstacle course.

Leave Niederkirchnerstrasse and follow Stresemannstrasse to Potsdamer Platz.

3 Potsdamer Platz

Once the heart of Berlin, Potsdamer Platz was totally destroyed by Allied bombing during World War II. When the Wall went up, this famous square remained a desolate wasteland. It had become a no-go area; redevelopment was impossible and, although underground trains passed from East to West, they didn't stop at Potsdamer Platz station. Reconstruction of the area with its impressive skyline has restored the place as a glamorous new version of the old. The European headquarters of electronics giant Sony crowned by a pavilion of sails shading William II's Kaisersaal represents one of Berlin's main characteristics: the juxtaposition of old world meeting new.

Walk up Ebertstrasse to the Brandenburger Tor.

4 From the Brandenburger Tor to the Reichstag

The Wall ran directly in front of the Gate before skirting the rear of the Reichstag. During the Cold War, Western politicians made a point of coming to this spot to draw attention to the significance of this most famous East–West divide. When reports came in of a relaxation of the border restrictions on 9 November 1989, it was to this point that the crowd headed for celebration. At the northeastern corner of the Reichstag building, near the river, is a modest line of inscribed white crosses, the 'Memorial to the Victims of War and Violence'.

Follow the Reichstag-Ufer, then the Kronprinzen-Ufer westwards to Moltke Brücke (bridge).

5 River crossings

The border between East and West ran across the Spree a little way downstream from the ornate sandstone Moltke bridge (*see p36*), named after the victorious general of the Wars of Unification. (Note the bellicose cherubs sporting martial gear.) Berlin's waterways were a favourite means of escape in the early days of the Wall's history, but not all attempts were successful – the first death was recorded in August 1961, when Gunter Litfin was shot by East German border guards while trying to swim across the Teltow canal. Immediately barriers and booby traps were lowered into the water to deter others, while patrol boats monitored the entire network. This did not prevent the crew of a passenger steamer from hijacking their own ship and navigating it safely to the Western bank, after getting the captain drunk and locking him in his cabin.

Walk: Nikolai Quarter

This walk takes you through the heart of the old centre of Berlin.

Allow 1 hour.

From Alexanderplatz station, walk southwest through Alexanderplatz. Cross Spandauer Strasse to the square opposite.

1 'Marx–Engels Forum'/Forum an der Rathausstrasse

Two massive, monolithic bronze statues of the famous Socialist prophets occupy central position in this otherwise unremarkable expanse, which is a park only in the minds of the planners. After the Wall had come down, someone spray-painted the following 'apology' on to the plinth: 'Sorry, but it's not our fault. Maybe next time things will turn out better.'

Return to Spandauer Strasse and turn right into Am Nussbaum.

2 Nikolaiviertel (The Nikolai Quarter)

In the 1980s, the East German authorities finally got around to recreating this historic quarter of the city, once the heart of the twin settlements of Berlin-Cölln. Most of the original buildings, including the 13th-century church now at the centre of the refashioned 'quarter', were reduced to rubble during World War II, and the present appearance of the district is only reminiscent of the original.

Nevertheless, with its narrow cobbled streets (mercifully traffic-free) and restored houses, the Nikolai Quarter is a pleasant place in which to stroll and relax. Although there is housing here for more than 1,500 people, it is the tourist whose needs are catered for. Pubs and restaurants abound, and the prices in the shops put most locals off.

At the end of Am Nussbaum, pass Zum Nussbaum ('At the Nut Tree'), a restored pub whose name honours a 16th-century tavern. Circle the Nikolaikirche (*see pp79–80*), taking in Eiergasse, a street with a charming old-world flavour.

Turn left from the square in front of the church. On your left is the Knoblauchhaus.

3 Knoblauchhaus

The house was built by Johann Christian Knoblauch in 1759 and is one of the few buildings to have survived World War II. It is now a museum honouring the family after whom it is named. The Knoblauchs were prominent in Berlin society, supplying the university with a number of professors and the architect of the Neue Synagoge in Oranienburger Strasse. The Biedermeier room contains period furniture, and elsewhere in the house are documents, paintings and drawings. *Open: Tue–Sun 10am–6pm. Admission charge, free on Wed.*

Turn left on Poststrasse to reach Ephraim Palais.

4 Ephraim Palais

See pp49–50. Continue to Muhlendamm and turn right onto Spreeufer.

5 Spreeufer

The view across the Spree from the café terraces of the Ephraim Palace and Knoblauchhaus is not picturesque. Move on quickly and the spell cast by the Nikolai Quarter will not be broken! *Turn right into Rathausstrasse and right again into Poststrasse. This brings you back to the central square.*

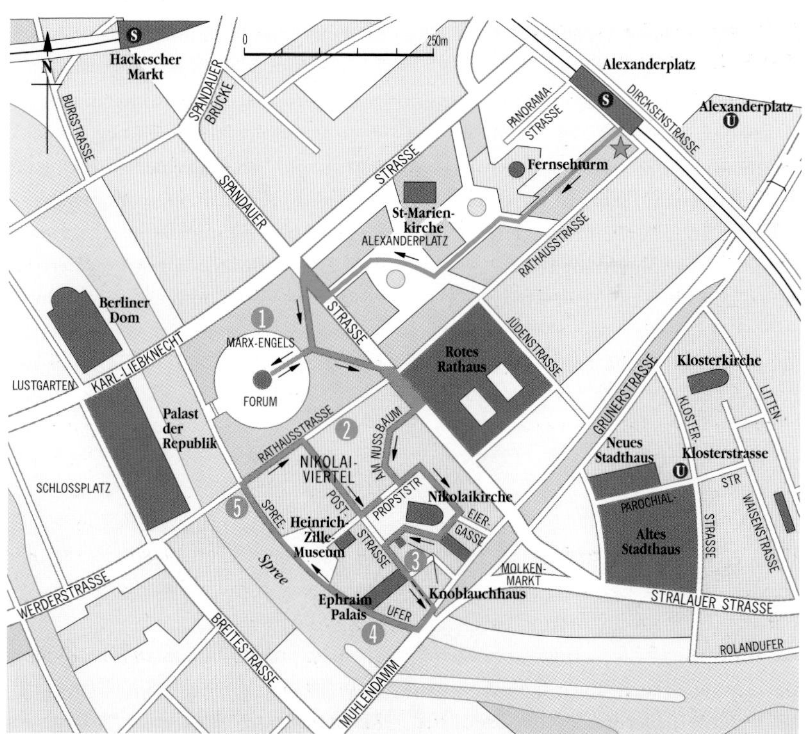

Walk: Kreuzberg

This walk explores the heart of one of Berlin's most cosmopolitan and exciting districts, the centre of the city's 'alternative' culture and the home of the Turkish community (see p16).

Allow about 1 to 1½ hours.

Start at Kottbusser Tor U-Bahn station.

1 Kottbusser Tor

Welcome to Kreuzberg! The 'Mountain of the Cross' which gives the area its name is a small hill in what is now Viktoria Park. Factories began to overrun the vineyards which once grew around the slopes of the hill early in the 19th century, and parts of the district still have an industrial character. During the revolution of 1848 Kreuzberg was a centre of working-class resistance, of street protests and machine-breaking. The population was dragooned into the barrack housing known as *Mietskasernen*; ever since, Kreuzberg has been one of the most densely populated of Berlin's districts. 'Kotti' is typical of radical Kreuzberg where crumbling 19th-century apartment blocks alternate with equally fast-fading 1960s architecture, where all-night bars illuminate the shadows of the U-Bahn girders. The atmosphere is exotic, suggesting both excess and the

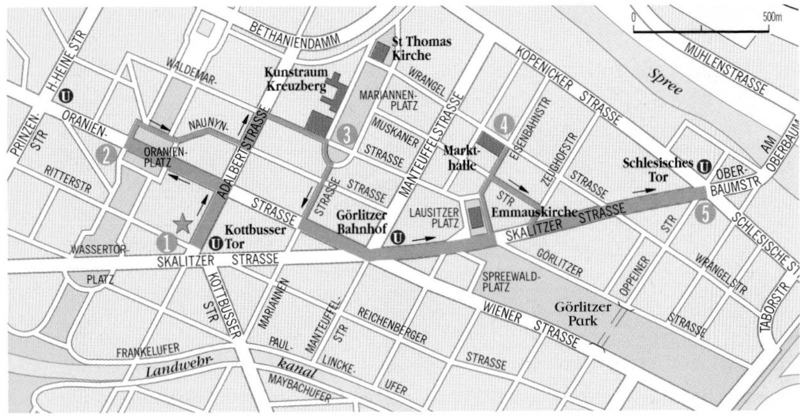

unexpected. About a third of Berlin's 140,000 Turks live in Kreuzberg. Just across the canal from Kottbusser Tor, on Maybachufer, is the Turkish market, an outdoor community centre where the locals gather to exchange gossip, read Turkish-language newspapers and listen to Turkish radio stations. This is also the place to buy fresh figs, dates, spices and peppers.

Walk up Adalbertstrasse. Turn left into Oranienstrasse to Oranienplatz.

2 Oranienplatz

Oranienplatz is in many ways the most attractive part of East Kreuzberg, its sedate gardens surrounded by elegant 19th-century apartments. As the main artery, Oranienstrasse is best explored by hopping on and off the No 129 bus.

Leave Oranienplatz via Naunynstrasse (the house murals are worth looking out for) and Adalbertstrasse, then turn right into Waldemarstrasse. At the square, turn right again into Mariannenstrasse.

3 Mariannenplatz

This is a favourite square with Kreuzbergers, who seem to delight in its slightly worn appearance. It was laid out as a garden by Peter Joseph Lenné (of Tiergarten and Charlottenburg fame) in 1853.

The yellow-brick building with its twin pencil-like towers on the west side of the square is the Kunstraum Kreuzberg. It was built as a hospital in the 1840s and has been converted into a first-rate cultural centre with studios, workshops, exhibition and concert rooms, and a Turkish bookshop. The Künstlerhaus (modern art gallery) here is the best place to take the cultural pulse of Kreuzberg.

On the north side is the Church of St Thomas, which used to stand in the shadow of the Wall. It was completed in 1869 by a pupil of Schinkel's, F Adler. On the south side is a jocular sculpture by D Wolff and G Jendritzko called *Fallen of the Berlin Fire Brigade*, depicting a couple of firemen firing water hoses at one another.

Tel: (030) 902 981455.

Open: Tue–Sun noon–7pm.

Turn left on to Oranienstrasse and continue along Skalitzer Strasse. Turn left along the eastern side of Lausiter Platz and right into Eisenbahnstrasse.

4 Markthalle

This colourful weekday market caters for the locals, selling vegetables, cheese and fruit.

Retrace your steps and turn left down Muskaner Strasse, then right on Zeughofstrasse. Turn left on Skalitzer Strasse to Schlesisches Tor U-Bahn.

5 Schlesisches Tor

The square which occupies the site of the old Silesian Gate now marks the eastern frontier of Kreuzberg. Architectural buffs will enjoy the *Jugendstil* station which dates from 1902 and was one of the original stations on the first U-Bahn line, known today as the Orient Express.

Walk: Prenzlauer Berg

This walk explores Berlin's most famous old working-class district, now becoming a favourite night haunt with its restaurants, cafés and bars.

Allow 2 hours.

Start at Schönhauser Allee U-Bahn station.

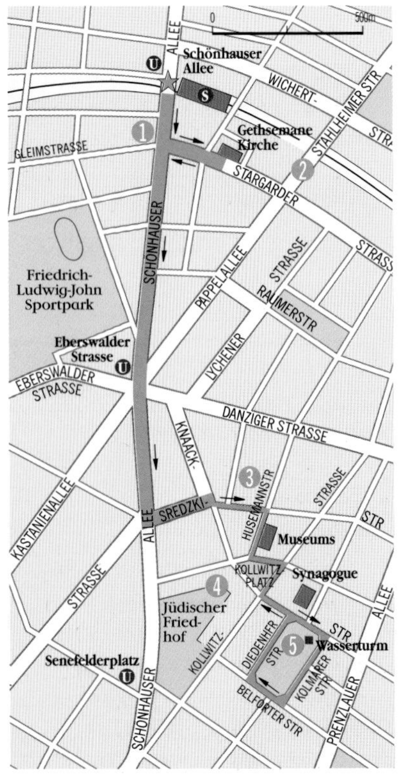

1 Schlesisches Tor

A good spot to sample Prenzlauer Berg's new, upmarket image. Neglected after the war, this district gained a reputation in the 1960s and 1970s for gritty radical opposition to the GDR. As the fabric of its buildings continued to crumble, the squatters moved in. Attempts to renovate the area were already in progress before the Wall came down, but the process of rejuvenation has accelerated.

Around the station gathers a string of pizzerias, plush bars, smart restaurants, fashion boutiques and galleries, all in Kastanienallee.

Head down Schönhauser Allee and turn first left into Stargarder Strasse. On your left is the Gethsemane Kirche.

2 Gethsemane Kirche (Gethsemane Church)

The modest appearance of the plain red-brick church with the green spire belies its dramatic recent history. During the last days of the

Honecker regime, in the autumn of 1989, the Gethsemane Kirche became the unofficial headquarters of the democracy movement Neues Forum (New Forum). Hopeful faces lit by candlelight during nightly vigils for peace left an enduring impression on visitors, including the world media. *Continue down Schönhauser Allee, past the junction with Eberswalder Strasse, then turn left into Sredzkistrasse. On the corner are the former premises of Schultheiss' brewery, dating from 1891, now fully restored and offering galleries, cinemas and a Bavarian restaurant called* Leopold's. *Turn right into Husemannstrasse.*

3 Husemannstrasse

With its windmills and open rolling fields, Prenzlauer Berg was once Berlin's bread basket. All this changed with the coming of industry in the 19th century, as a result of which the district acquired the unenviable reputation of having the largest population density per building in the world. Workers were packed like sardines into *Mietskasernen*, vast, six-storey lodging houses whose once elegant façades hid a grim succession of cramped and gloomy back courtyards. The renovation of Husemannstrasse began in the 1980s and is almost complete. It marks the beginning of a revitalised café life with a trendy, upmarket feel not popular with all the locals.

The Wasserturm

4 Kollwitzplatz

The square is named after the artist Käthe Kollwitz (1861–1945), who lived nearby in a house since demolished. Children play unselfconsciously around her statue in the middle of the square, which is how she would have liked it. A favourite local nightspot is Restauration 1900, a rather chic café-restaurant. *Turn left on to Knaackstrasse. On your right is a garden.*

5 Wasserturm (Water Tower)

Now converted into apartments, the polygonal tower was opened as a sanitary measure in 1875. The Nazis found a more sinister use for it – it became a prison for torturing and murdering Social Democrats and Communists, who offered strong resistance in Prenzlauer Berg. *Return to Kollwitzplatz. The nearest U-Bahn station is Senefelderplatz.*

Walk: Sachsenhausen

This walk, more in the manner of a pilgrimage, takes in one of the most notorious of the Nazi concentration camps.

Allow 3 hours.

Start at Oranienburg S-Bahn station (line 1, to the north of the city). Turn right into Stralsunder Strasse, then into Bernauer Strasse. Turn left into Strasse der Einheit and right into Strasse der Nationen.

Sachsenhausen Concentration Camp

The concentration camp was opened in July 1936 at the same time as Berlin was hosting the Olympic Games. By the end of World War II more than 220,000 prisoners had passed through the gates; tens of thousands had been murdered or had died from illness and neglect. The victims included political opponents, Jews, Soviet POWs, homosexuals, gypsies, criminals and other 'anti-social elements'. In 1945, the Soviet secret service took over Sachsenhausen as an internment camp for their own prisoners – an estimated 12,000 of them perished.

The future of Sachsenhausen is a highly sensitive issue. The original buildings and structural remains are 'guarantors of the memory', therefore their preservation and restoration are of utmost priority. In recent years several buildings have been restored. Small permanent exhibitions which address the significant aspects of the history of these sites have been installed and others will follow.

International Museum (No 2)

The history of the Jews in Sachsenhausen is told through photographs and artefacts. There is also a section on the forgery and printing press which the Nazis developed here in a vain attempt to subvert the British and US economies.

The original gate of the camp has the soothing look of a provincial railway station. (The slogan *Arbeit macht frei* means 'Work Makes You Free'.)

Appellplatz (No 4)

Pass through to the concrete exercise yard, with a view of the watchtowers, the perimeter wall and the barbed wire electrified fence. Three times a day the prisoners were herded on to this square for roll call and to witness executions on the camp gallows.

Cell block (No 6)

This simple white-washed building was once used to detain prisoners of war. Some of the cells have been restored; others, including that belonging to the German resistance leader Pastor Martin Niemöller, have been converted into shrines with wreaths.

Camp Museum (No 8)

In the former prison kitchens, this is an exhibition of life in the camp with models and a reconstruction of the tiered bunks on which prisoners had to sleep.

Memorial (No 10)

A simple concrete obelisk carved with inverted triangles, commemorating the 18 categories of prisoner.

Station Z (No 12)

Only the brick foundations remain of the notorious extermination centre. Soviet prisoners of war were executed here – some 18,000 of them, each believing he was being taken for a 'medical examination'. Behind the wall with the eye chart was an SS soldier who fired a shot into the prisoner's neck through a concealed aperture. The bodies were later disposed of in the adjoining crematorium. Also on the premises was a gas chamber and execution ditch (No 11).

Pathology Department (No 15)

Corpses were brought here for dissection and experiment. Gold was removed from teeth and sold, and tattooed skin was made into handbags or lampshades. The cellar in which the bodies were stored can also be visited.

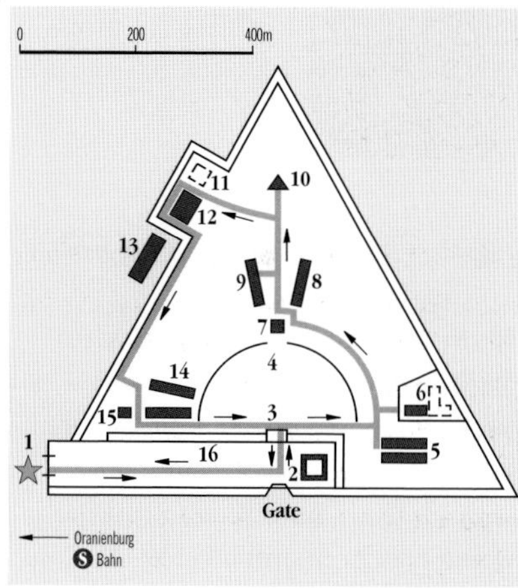

SITE PLAN

1 Entrance
2 International Museum
3 Tower 'A'
4 Appellplatz
5 Restored barracks
6 Underground cells and prison
7 Site of gallows
8 Camp Museum (formerly kitchen)
9 Cinema (formerly laundry)
10 Memorial
11 Execution ditch
12 Station Z
13 Exhibition hall
14 Infirmary and morgue
15 Pathology Department
16 Restored camp wall and electrified fence

Open: Apr–Sept 8am–6pm; Oct–Mar 9am–4.30pm. Closed: Mon. Free admission.

Tour: Bus 100

See Berlin's tourist landmarks, East and West, from one of the city's famous double-decker buses (they leave every 10 minutes) – and avoid paying a small fortune. An ideal introduction to the city. See pp20–21 for route.

Allow about 1 hour.

Board at Bahnhof Zoologischer Garten.

From the Zoo to the Tiergarten

The Berlin bus company BVG calls route 100 its 'red thread' from Bahnhof Zoo to Alexanderplatz. Before 1989, such a journey from West to East Berlin would have been unthinkable – the Wall would have seen to that. On your left as you travel along busy Budapester Strasse a pair of stone elephants guards the main entrance to Berlin Zoo, while on the right is Berlin's premier shopping mecca, the Europa-Center – also handy for entertainment and tourist information. The next major port of call is Lützow Platz, which is where to get off for the Bauhaus-Archiv (*see p30*), a museum devoted to the famous 1920s school of architecture founded by Walter Gropius. The bus now heads north into the Tiergarten, once a hunting ground for the Electors (*Tier* means 'animal') and now an attractive park (*see pp96–7 & 132–3*). Directly ahead, at the far end of Hofjäger Allee, is one of Berlin's best-known monuments, the Siegessäule (Victory Column – *see p85*). The golden figure on top is known to Berliners as 'Gold Else'.

From the Tiergarten to the Brandenburger Tor

The bus continues through the Tiergarten towards the River Spree. The stately building on the left is Schloss Bellevue, an 18th-century palace which is also the official residence of the President of the Republic. Also on the left-hand side is the exhibition hall now known as Haus der Kulturen der Welt (*see p59*). As the bus passes through Platz der Republik, the monumental parliament building, the Reichstag, looms into view (*see pp80–81*). As the bus turns right into Friedrich Ebert Strasse, it follows the route of the former Berlin Wall. Directly ahead is Berlin's most famous monument, the Brandenburg Gate (*see p33*). When the Wall was in place, this was the most potent symbol of German division. Nowadays it stands for German unity and hopefully for peace, the original intention when it was conceived in 1788.

Through the heart of Imperial Berlin

The lime trees which give Unter den Linden its name are still in place, but there is no sign now of the military parades that used to pass up and down here in the days of the Kaisers. The first major intersection is Friedrichstrasse, Berlin's red-light district before World War I and still a centre of entertainment today. The sequence of majestic architectural set pieces which gave Imperial Berlin its unique character begins on the left with the State Library and the Humboldt University. Next in line is the Neue Wache, or guardhouse (*see p79*), and the Zeughaus (Arsenal), now the Deutsches Historisches Museum (German History Museum). The massive domed building coming up on the left is the Protestant Cathedral commissioned by Kaiser William II, who used to wave to the crowds from the balcony of the Stadtschloss (City Palace), which once stood opposite.

From Karl-Liebknecht-Strasse to Alexanderplatz

To the left of the Cathedral is Museumsinsel (Museum Island – *see pp72–8*). The No 100 bus completes its journey by circling Alexanderplatz ('Alex' to locals), once the main square of East Berlin and now extensively redeveloped. Take the lift to the top of the 368m- (1,207ft-) high Fernsehturm (TV tower – *see p50*) for spectacular views of the city, or return to base via the U-Bahn or S-Bahn – both networks have stations on Alexanderplatz.

Museum Island – Berlin's cultural centre

Tour: Boat trips

In the summer months taking a boat trip is a wonderful way to explore the River Spree and the extensive waterways that flow into it to the west and to the east of the city. Various shipping companies offer a wide range of tours to suit different interests.

TOUR 1
From Tegel to Wannsee

The Greenwich-Promenade is close to Tegel Park (U-Bahn Tegel). The boat sails across the broad expanses of the Tegeler See before weaving its way through the islands which mark the juncture with the Havel. The first major port of call is Spandau; the magnificent Zitadelle or fort with its 16th-century bastion, the Juliusturm, is clearly visible from the bridge. This is where the Havel and the Spree join forces. The boat opts for the narrow neck of the Havel, heading for Freybrücke and the marshy promontory known as the Tiefwerder. Here the Havel widens again and to the left there are marvellous views of the vast Grunewald Forest as the boat heads towards the smart villas of Kladow. Disembark at Pfaueninsel (Peacock Island) to explore the nature reserve conceived as a love nest for Frederick William II and his mistress, the Countess Lichtenau. Pick up line 2 at the pier opposite the island. The boat now passes under the Glienickebrücke, linking Berlin and Potsdam, the scene of a number of spy-swaps during the Cold War. The next stretch of river takes in Volkspark Klein-Glienicke and Park Babelsburg before navigating the headland at Griebnitzsee. The tour finishes several stops further on at Wannsee pier, not far from the S-Bahn station.

Stern und Kreisschiffahrt GmbH line 1 leaves from the Greenwich-Promenade in Tegel every day on the hour from 10am to 5pm; line 2 leaves from the Pier near Wannsee station every day on the half hour from 10.30am to 4.30pm. Journey time 6 to 8 hours.

TOUR 2
The city centre

Setting out from the Kongresshalle, the boat heads for the Reichstag building, which looms into view on the right bank. The smoothed-over expanse of terrain opposite was once part of the Berlin Wall death strip. Beyond the

STERN UND KREISSCHIFFAHRT GMBH

Puschkinallee 15, 12435, Berlin. Tel: (030) 536 3600. www.sternundkreis.de

Friedrichstrasse railway bridge is Museum Island (*see pp72–8*). The pretty Nikolai Quarter (*see pp104–5*) is on the left as the boat heads for the Mühlendamm lock. Several bridges on is the Oberbaumbrücke, where the counter-intelligence chief, Karla, crosses to the west at the climax of John Le Carré's novel *Smiley's People*. The boat now turns into the Landwehrkanal, passing through Kreuzberg (*see pp106–7*), the south side of the Tiergarten (*see pp96–7*) and Charlottenburg (*see pp39–42*), then back along the Spree to the Haus der Kulturen der Welt (*see p59*).

TOUR 3
Müggelsee

This tour's departure point is the Tiergarten pier, from where the boat follows the course of the Spree through the historic Mitte district. The area north of the Jannowitzbrücke is heavily industrialised. Before 1989 this was where the river formed the boundary between East and West, so the neighbouring districts of Friedrichshain on the left bank and Kreuzberg on the right were isolated from one another. The route continues through Treptow to the old town of Köpenick. Just beyond Schlossinsel is the medieval fishermen's quarter of Kietz. Formerly a popular holiday resort with East Berliners, the Grosser Müggelsee remains a natural sanctuary for wildlife (*see pp136–7*).

A cruise on the Havel makes a refreshing change from pounding the streets

The Spree

Rivers are the lifeblood of all great cities and Berlin is no exception. Slow-moving, at times almost torpid, its arteries prone to congealing with mud and silt, the River Spree is, on the face of it, a surprising source of urban greatness and prosperity. But the Spree has always had one great advantage: it is perfectly situated at the crossroads of major trade routes stretching in every direction – a factor which earned Berlin membership of the most powerful mercantile system of the Middle Ages, the Hanseatic League. With the coming of the Industrial Revolution, human intervention became necessary to adapt the Spree to new demands. Weirs, locks and canals began to appear along every stretch as the river was straightened and diverted to meet the needs of an increasing volume of barge traffic. The Landwehr Canal was completed in 1850, the Spandau Canal in 1859; by the turn of the 20th century additional waterways, such as the Teltow and the Hohenzollern, had joined the system. With the canals came the factories and their inevitable by-product, pollution. Once 'somewhat green in colour and clear', the Spree turned murky and sullen. But Berlin expanded and became wealthy at the river's expense: coal, building materials, iron and steel, and petroleum were transported in vast quantities – even today, the Spree carries more goods traffic than the railways.

This is an unassuming river with an almost unique capacity to surprise. Which visitor confronting the vista from the Westhafen docks, for example, would suspect that, simply by turning his back, he would encounter the dreamy tree-shrouded stretch which winds its way lazily towards Charlottenburg and the Tiergarten? Today, pleasure cruisers ply their trade alongside the barges in ever-increasing numbers, but the Spree will never cease to be what it has always been – a working river.

Moltke Bridge

The Spree – a river with a charm of its own

Excursions

There are several interesting places to visit, all within reach of the city centre. Take a trip to Brandenburg with its bustling Old Town and lovely cathedral, Potsdam with its three historic Hohenzollern palaces, the peaceful wooded waterland of Spreewald, or the old town of Wittenberg, famed for its monastery where the father of the Protestant Reformation, Martin Luther, began his protests.

BRANDENBURG

Some 62km (39 miles) west of Berlin, Brandenburg is the historic capital of the Mark of Brandenburg, a territory once on the frontier of the Holy Roman Empire. Despite wartime bombing, the medieval town is remarkably intact and is currently undergoing extensive restoration. The surrounding countryside is extremely attractive, with beautiful unspoilt woodland and lakes.
www.stadt-brandenburg.de

Neustadt (New Town)

To avoid the large and frankly ugly industrial suburb, leave the station via Grosse Gartenstrasse, then cross the bridge into Steinstrasse, at the bottom of which is one of two surviving city gates, the Steintortum. Exhibitions are sometimes held here. The large car park in Neustädtische Markt marks the beginning of the New Town, which is built on an island on the River Havel. It was founded in the late 12th century, not long after the 'old' town. On the southern side of the square, hemmed in by 1960s apartment blocks, is the **Katharinenkirche** (St Katherine's Church), a red-brick building with an ornate tower. The church is 15th century and there are wall paintings dating from this period behind the high altar, on the ceiling (note the donkey playing the bagpipes), and in the north and south chapels. The Aldermen chapel has a grille decorated with the Brandenburg crest and private pews originally intended for worshipping civic dignitaries. There is also a Baroque pulpit, gamely supported by the head of St Paul, dating from 1668.

TOURIST INFORMATION OFFICE

Steinstrasse 66–67, 14776 Brandenburg.
Tel: (03381) 208 769; fax: (03381) 208 774.
www.stadt-brandenburg.de or www.reiseland-brandenburg.de.
By train: from Hauptbahnhof, Friedrichstrasse and Zoologischer Garten.
By road: E51 and E30.

Town Museum – Frey Haus, Ritterstrasse 96. Tel: (03381) 522 048. Open: Wed–Fri 9am–5pm, Sat–Sun 10am–5pm. Admission charge.

Altstadt (Old Town)

Access to the Old Town is via Hauptstrasse, which crosses the omnipresent River Havel. The area is now pedestrianised, with coffee bars, pizzerias, market stalls and tourist information. At the far end is Altstädtische Markt, dominated by the late Gothic Rathaus (town hall), a sturdy brick structure with a stepped gable. Guarding it is the Brandenburger Roland, an oversized primitive statue. On Nikolaiplatz stands the other surviving town gate, in splendid isolation.

Dominsel (Cathedral Island)

Follow Mühlentorstrasse away from the town hall to Mühlendamm and Cathedral Island. This is the most attractive part of town: picturesque, quiet and secluded, the trees reflected in the calm waters of the Havel. The island was settled in the 10th century and a Romanesque cathedral dedicated to Saints Peter and Paul founded shortly afterwards. The nave, transepts and choir were later raised and vaulted to create more light and space. (See the exhibition in the porch.) The cathedral has an understated beauty; look out for the former high altar (1375), now in the south transept and inexplicably separated from the altar panels depicting the Crucifixion, which can still be seen in the chancel. The choir stalls are the work of a master artist, Hans the woodcarver, and the handsome Gothic wardrobe for storing vestments is another fine piece of craftsmanship. The cathedral organ, dating from 1723 to 1725 and boasting 2,000 pipes, is one of the best preserved in Germany. On your way out, don't miss the Dom Café with its tasty selection of home-made *Kuchen* (cakes) – closed on Mondays.

Also in Brandenburg

Angelika Schmidt-Thielemann's fabric shop and café on Steinstrasse 21 sells

Brandenburg's Old Town

chair cushions, tablecloths, curtains and clothing, made using the age-old technique of printing with woodblocks, then adding indigo dye.

Marienberg Hill (Altstadt) is a park with fine views of the town, especially from the look-out tower. There is also an open-air swimming pool and theatre.

Lake Beetzsee, near Dominsel, is a popular venue for regattas. Boat trips are available to the many lakes, and even as far as Potsdam and Berlin.

POTSDAM

In 1993 Potsdam celebrated its 1,000th anniversary; its importance, however, dates from the early 18th century, when it became a garrison town and the summer residence of the Hohenzollerns. Now it is the capital of the federal state of Brandenburg.

Altstadt (Old Town)

Sadly, many of the buildings which comprised the core of the Old Town, including the Schloss and the Garrison Church, were destroyed during World War II. Among the survivors, to the left of the Lange Brücke, is the elongated, red-brick façade of the Marstall, designed by Johann Nering in 1685. Rearing sculptures of horses indicate that this was once the royal stables, now the **Filmmuseum**. On the opposite side of the bridge is the **Nikolaikirche** (St Nicholas Church). The fortress-like base is the work of Ludwig Persius and dates from the 1830s. Schinkel added the dome ten years later. Much more

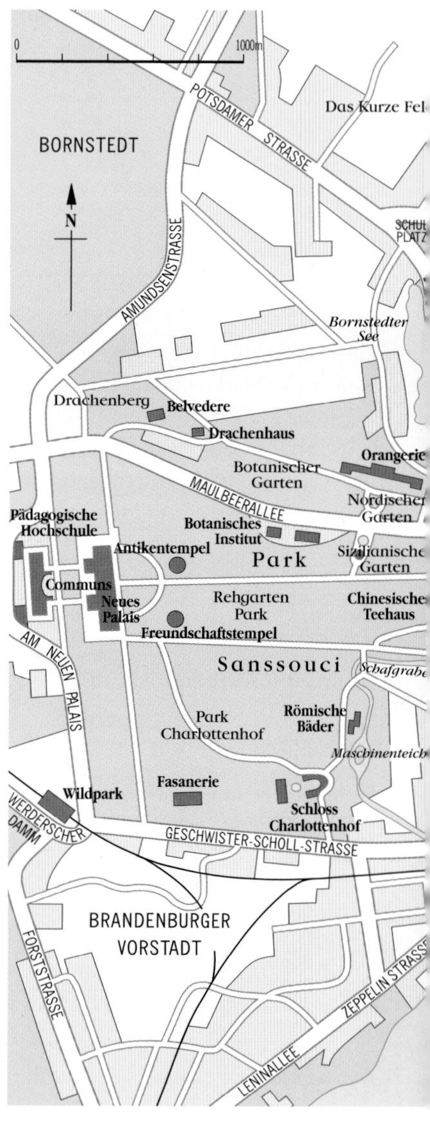

appealing is the beautifully proportioned Old Town Hall, just to the right, completed in 1753 and now an arts centre (**Kulturhaus**).

Potsdam and Sanssouci

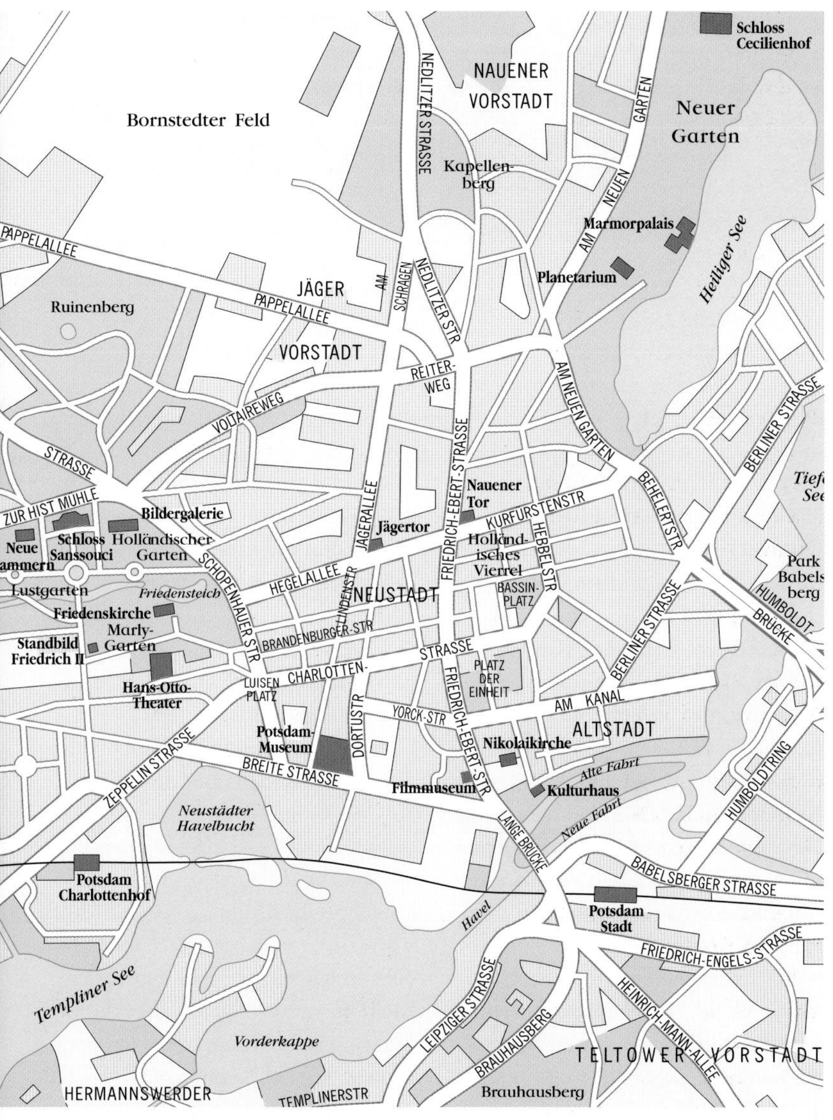

Potsdam Museum: Breite Strasse 13. Tel: (0331) 289 6803. Open: Tue–Sun 9am–5pm. Admission charge.
Filmmuseum: Marstall am Lustgarten, Breite Strasse 1A. Tel: (0331) 271 812. www.filmmuseum-potsdam.de. Open: daily 10am–6pm. Admission charge.
Kulturhaus: Am Alten Markt.

The ornate exterior of the palace at Sanssouci

Tel: (0331) 293 175.
Nikolaikirche open: Mon 2–5pm, Tue–Sat 10am–5pm, Sun 11.30am–5pm. Free admission.

Neustadt (New Town) and Holländisches Viertel (Dutch Quarter)

In 1732 Frederick William II ordered the building of a new town running north of Platz der Einheit (Unity Square). Neustadt, the result, is the most attractive part of Potsdam to have survived.

Two foreign communities lived in the Neustadt and Holländisches Viertel: the Huguenot presence is recalled by Johann Boumann's French Church dating from 1753, while construction workers from Holland, employed in building the new town, were housed in the aptly named Holländisches Viertel. Several streets of red-brick, gabled houses were built to accommodate the Dutch workers, and survive to this day.

The Nauener Tor and the Jägertor, which are situated further to the north, are two surviving town gates. The former, with its yellow circular towers, reveals Frederick II's sometimes wayward architectural taste.

Brandenburgerstrasse, with the 'other' Brandenburg Gate set at one end, has now been pedestrianised and is crowded and busy with shoppers. There is an altogether different atmosphere in the quieter, more secluded Lindenstrasse, which has a modest, understated charm.

Schloss Cecilienhof

Bus 695 leaves from outside the Landkreisamt Rathaus and takes the visitor through the **Neuer Garten** (New Garden), a park laid out after 1786 by Frederick William II. It owes its present appearance to Lenné, who also landscaped the Berlin Tiergarten. Half hidden among the trees are the Marble Palace, the Chinese Shingle House and the Orangery, all of which date from the 18th century.

In total contrast to the park buildings is the Schloss itself, modelled on an English Tudor manor house and commissioned by Kaiser William II for his son and daughter-in-law.

Schloss Cecilienhof is famous for the Potsdam Conference, which took place here in 1945. Among the dignitaries attending the conference were the 'big three': Winston Churchill of Great Britain, Harry S Truman of the United States and Joseph Stalin of the Soviet Union. The conference eventually redrew the post-war map of Europe, with profound consequences that are still being felt today.

The rooms in which the delegations met privately, as well as the conference hall itself, may be visited (an English-language leaflet tells the story of the conference in more detail).
Neuer Garten. Tel: (0331) 969 4202. Open: May–Oct, Tue–Sun 9am–5pm. Admission charge.

Schloss Sanssouci

Sanssouci means 'carefree', and it was to escape the burdens of kingship that Frederick the Great built this idyllic summer residence for himself from 1745 to 1747. The architect was his friend Georg Wenzeslaus von Knobelsdorff, who also designed the new wing of the Charlottenburg Palace (*see pp41–2*). Only group tours of the palace apartments are permitted and the demand can be excessive in the summer season, sometimes leading to disappointment.

Sanssouci is a modest, single-storey affair, although the rococo interior is sumptuous, with its marble floors, stuccoed ceilings, richly upholstered furniture, sculptures, precious vases and elegant clocks. Highlights are the study and bedroom of Frederick the Great, the concert chamber, and the elliptical Marble Hall with its Corinthian columns of Carrara marble. Of the guest rooms, the fourth, known as the 'Voltaire room', is the most interesting. The great French philosopher is said to have stayed here between 1750 and 1753, while attending Frederick's court as an ambassador of the Enlightenment, but despite helping the king to write a treatise on the ideal ruler, Voltaire

Traffic has been outlawed from the centre of Potsdam's New Town

Detail from the Chinese Tea House

became disillusioned with the wilful Prussian monarch, who in turn said of his erstwhile advisor: 'he has the slyness and will of an ape'.

Adjoining the palace is the art gallery. The collection is sadly depleted but there are works by Van Dyck, Rubens and Caravaggio.

Tel: (0331) 969 4202. www.spsg.de. Open: Tue–Sun, tours every 20 minutes, 9am–12.30pm & 1–5pm. Admission charge. Picture Gallery open: Wed–Sun 9–11.45am & 12.30–4pm. Admission charge.

The gardens

The park is one of the most attractive features of the palace. Six terraces lead to the Great Fountain. To the east are the Obelisk Portal, the original entrance to the park, dating from 1748, and the Neptune Grotto (1753). On the other side of Hauptweg is the Friedenskirche (Church of Peace), a mausoleum built by Ludwig Persius for Frederick William IV in 1845 and modelled on an early Christian basilica. Among the figures adorning the roof of the **Chinesisches Teehaus** (Chinese Tea House) is a large monkey with the features of Voltaire – Frederick's revenge on his recalcitrant minister! Closer to the Maulbeerallee are the **Neue Kammern** (New Chambers) of 1771 to 1774 and the **Sizilianischer Garten** (Sicilian Garden), a Mediterranean fantasy of palm trees, fountains and exotic plants laid out by P J Lenné in 1857.

Conceived in the manner of a Renaissance palace, the stupendous **Orangerie** dates from 1851 to 1864. Terraces and staircases conspire with the elongated colonnade to overwhelm the visitor. The most famous guests to stay in the lavish guest rooms were Tsar Nicholas I of Russia and his consort, Princess Charlotte of Prussia. The Drachenhaus café, a delightful folly in the style of a Chinese pagoda, makes a suitable stopping-off point before returning to the Hauptweg and the New Palace.

Chinesisches Teehaus tel: (0331) 969 4222. Open: 15 May–15 Oct, Tue–Sun 10am–5pm. Admission charge.
Neue Kammern tel: (0331) 969 4202. Open: 1 Apr–14 May, Tue–Sun 10am–5pm. Admission charge.
Orangerie tel: (0331) 969 4280. Open: 15 May–15 Oct, Tue–Sun 10am– 5pm. Admission charge.

Neues Palais (New Palace)
This massive Baroque edifice, its three storeys of red brick divided by a series of enormous pilasters surrounded by a balustrade and central cupola, could hardly be more different from Sanssouci. It was constructed between 1763 and 1769 for Frederick the Great by Johann Buring, responsible for the exterior, and Carl von Gontard, who took over in 1764. Apart from the guest apartments, there are ballrooms, reception rooms and a theatre, while at the back of the building are entirely separate accommodation quarters for servants and courtiers known as the Communs.

There are group tours of Frederick's apartments, including the music chamber (Frederick was an accomplished flautist), study, dining room and library. At present some parts of the palace are in a slightly worn state, the result of years of neglect.

TOURIST INFORMATION OFFICE

Am Neuen Markt 1, 14467 Potsdam. Tel: (0331) 275 580. www.potsdamtourismus.de.
By train: S-Bahn line 3 via Wannsee to Potsdam Stadt.
By road: E51.

The New Palace is an overwhelming Baroque presence

Open: 1 Apr–31 Oct Sat–Thur 9am–5pm; 1 Nov–31 Mar 9am–4pm.

SPREEWALD

An area of outstanding natural beauty lying about 100km (62 miles) southeast of Berlin, the Spreewald is the perfect antidote to the hectic life of the capital. Slav settlers arrived here in the 7th century and they never regretted it – their successors, the Sorbs, still live here today and speak a language with clear affinities with Polish or Russian. The Romantic poet Achim von Arnim visited the Spreewald in 1817 and sang its praises to his wife Bettina. More than 40 years later the novelist Theodor Fontane discovered the forests and waterways, likening the latter in his travelogue, *Wanderungen durch die Mark Brandenburg*, to Venice in the days of its infancy. But it was left to the notorious financial speculator Bethel Henry Strousberg to make the Spreewald accessible to 19th-century Berliners. Strousberg built a railway line from the Görlitzer Bahnhof to Cottbus and then founded a newspaper to recommend the region's attractions. Today, tourists and Berliners alike flock here in their thousands, but as the Spreewald extends for more than 700sq km (270sq miles) there should be room for everyone.

Exploring the canals in Spreewald is a relaxing way to enjoy the area

The region is comprised of two halves: the **Unterspreewald** and the **Oberspreewald**. The scenery is more striking in the Oberspreewald, which extends south of Lübbenau. Here the Spree fragments into dozens of sluggish tributaries, feeding an astonishingly complex network of water channels and canals. The former irrigate the market gardens, which are everywhere, producing onions, gherkins, beetroot, and the like, while the latter serve as roads, carrying the produce to market and the local children to school. Boat travel is not the only means of transportation, but for most people it is the most enjoyable way to see the truly remarkable scenery. The banks of the waterways heave under weeping willow, poplar and ash; marsh plants and tall grasses provide cover for white storks, waterfowl, and even grass snakes, while the Spree's countless arteries yield prodigious quantities of eel, pike and perch, destined for the dining tables of local inns and guesthouses. Further afield there is more to discover – enormous rounded haystacks resembling primitive huts, wooden-framed houses with the distinctive crossed-serpent pattern on their gables, village churches, ancient fortifications, craft shops and museums.

The history, customs and traditions of the local Sorb population, still very much alive, are fascinating and worth exploring.

Lübbenau

For information on boat trips (by paddle boat or punt), visit the tourist office (*Fremdenverkehrsamt*) at Poststrasse 25, or follow the signs advertising *Kahnfahrten* or *Paddelboote.* Lübbenau itself has a charming old town centre, which tends to get very crowded in season. Points of interest include the Marktplatz and the 18th-century church of St Nicholas; the Schloss, which dates from the Napoleonic period; and the **Spreewald Museum** nearby, which provides a useful introduction to the region.
Spreewald Museum open: May–Oct, Tue–Sun 10am–5pm. Admission charge.

Lübben

The mainly Baroque Paul-Gerhard-Kirche is worth seeing, as is the much older (and smaller) Steinkirchen (stone church) dating from the beginning of the 13th century. Lübben also has its own Schloss and modest fortifications.
Bus from Lübbenau or train from Berlin Lichtenberg.

Train from Berlin-Lichterfelde (journey time 1 hour, irregular service).

Severin-Kuhn (*Ku'damm 216, tel: (030) 880 4190. www.severin-kuehn-berlin.de*) offers a **coach tour** to Lübbenau which lasts seven hours and includes a **boat ride**.

If you are driving, take road B96. For further information apply to the regional tourist board: Fremdenverkehrsamt Lübbenau, *Ehm-Welk-Str 15, 0322 Lübbenau/Spreewald. Tel: (03542) 3668; fax: (03542) 46770.*

Spreewald: a landscape to inspire an artist

Lehde

The **Freilichtsmuseum** (open-air museum) describes the history and customs of the area and provides a fascinating insight into how the local farmhouses were constructed on the marshy ground.
30-minute walk from Lübbenau. Freilichtsmuseum open: Apr–Oct, Tue–Sun 10am–5pm. Admission charge.

Burg

Remote and therefore secluded, the local farmhouses here are the main attraction and there are good views from the Bismarckturm on top of the

Schlossberg, just a couple of kilometres from the village.
Bus from Lübben (40km/25 miles).

WITTENBERG (LUTHERSTADT WITTENBERG)

The name says it all. It was Martin Luther, then a university professor and monk, who put Wittenberg on the map in 1517 when he nailed his 95 theses to the door of the castle church, precipitating the Reformation, one of the most profound religious upheavals in history. On the corner of Martin-Luther-Strasse is the **Luther Oak**, commemorating the spot where, in December 1520, Father Martin publicly defied the Pope by burning the Papal Bull that threatened him with excommunication. In the 16th century Wittenberg was already famous for its university – both Shakespeare's Hamlet and Marlowe's Dr Faustus were students here. Scholars flocked to Wittenberg from all over Europe, outnumbering the permanent residents.

Martin Luther, the hero of Wittenberg, is commemorated in the Marktplatz

Lutherhalle

Luther's former monastery, the Lutherhalle on Collegienstrasse, is now a museum. Pass through the outer building into the imposing courtyard. Ahead is an immaculate white building with gabled roof, octagonal tower and an exquisite oriel window. The entrance is through a Renaissance doorway, the Katharinen-Portal, a birthday present from Luther to his wife in 1540. The highlight of the museum is Luther's private apartments which he shared with his wife, the former nun Katharina von Bora, and six children. Period furnishings, paintings, decorated wood panelling, and unusual items such as the tiled Renaissance stove in Luther's study convey the homeliness of Luther's family life. The other rooms on the first floor trace the dramatic life of the religious reformer and set it in the social and political context of the times. Aspects of the Catholic faith to which Luther later took exception – the proliferation of relics and the sale of indulgences – are illustrated by contemporary artefacts. There is also a copy of the Papal Bull of excommunication of 1520, a set of monks' robes, and an absorbing and highly amusing assortment of anti-Papal propaganda. Famous artists such as Dürer, Holbein and Lucas Cranach the Elder were recruited for a highly professional campaign which concentrated on spreading the Lutheran message through the printed word. Support from intellectual big guns at the university, such as Phillip Melanchthon, and the protection of the Elector, Frederick the Wise, saved Luther from the stake, but only after he had spent several months on the run, adopting the alias Junke Jorg. On his triumphant return, Wittenberg became a centre of Lutheran religious experiment and the exhibition highlights some of the more striking aspects, the new priestly uniform and an experimental liturgy, for example.

Lutherhalle in Wittenberg

The ground floor is something of a miscellany. There is a concert hall with a fine vaulted ceiling – this was once the monks' refectory. Elsewhere is an exhibition on the history of the museum and on Wittenberg's historic links with printing, while the cellar contains a collection of medallions and coins, including a medal of Luther struck in 1521.

Tel: (03491) 2671. Open: Tue–Sun 9am–5pm. Admission charge.

Wittenberg Town

In Luther's day the population of Wittenberg was only 2,000 and the entire length of the town stretched for less than a mile. The focal point is the stately and extremely photogenic Marktplatz with its magnificent, beautifully preserved town hall, a white gabled building with an ornate portal dating from the 16th century. At that time it was the centre of town life with shops, a hall for dancing and concerts, and a tavern. The canopied statues framing it are – inevitably – of Luther and Melanchthon, the former by the Berlin architects Schadow and Schinkel and dating from 1821. Dwarfing the houses on one side of the square are the twin towers of the **Stadtkirche St Marien**.

The 13th-century Town Church is Wittenberg's oldest building. Luther preached here and it was the first religious building to be adapted to the new Protestant rite. Its greatest artistic treasure is the large altar panel executed by the two Lucas Cranachs (elder and younger) and completed in 1547.
Stadtkirche St Marien open: daily, 10am–noon & 2–5pm.
Free admission.

Cranachhaus

The artist Lucas Cranach the Elder lived and worked here from 1513 to 1550, not only as a painter – he was also an apothecary, a publisher, the owner of a printing press, a town councillor and even mayor! The extremely picturesque house and courtyard were only recently rescued from falling into ruin. There is a gallery and wine bar at the rear.

Melanchthonhaus

Luther's second in command, famed throughout Europe as a humanist and Greek scholar, lived in this immaculately restored Renaissance house from 1536 to 1560. Stroll through the refurbished rooms, which include Melanchthon's study, and the period 'feel' is undeniable. The house is also a museum of university life, with student uniforms and fashion accessories from the 19th century. A more grisly exhibit is the hand of Susanne Zimmermann, who was broken on the wheel in 1728 for poisoning her stepchildren. Best to end on a happier note, and look at the garden where Frau Melanchthon was fond of growing herbs – part of the town wall is visible from here.
Open: Tue–Sun 9am–5pm.
Admission charge.

WITTENBERG INFORMATION

Schlossplatz 2, 06886 Lutherstadt, Wittenberg.
Tel: (03491) 498 610; fax: (03491) 498 611.
www.wittenberg.de. Open: Mon–Fri 9am–6.30pm, Sat–Sun 10am–4pm.
By train: every 2 hours from Bahnhof Berlin-Lichtenberg.
By road: E51/A9 to Coswig, then left on the B187.

Schlosskirche

It was to the door of this, the castle church, that Martin Luther nailed his 95 theses on 31 October 1517. Sadly, both church and door were destroyed by soldiers during the Seven Years' War (1760). The present building is 19th-century and looks it, from the inside at least. Luther and Melanchthon are both buried here, and replacement bronze doors, dating from 1858, commemorate the reformer's historic action. Climb the steps of the tower for splendid views over the River Elbe and surrounding countryside.

Open: daily 10am–noon & 2–5pm.
Free admission.

Martin Luther, instigator of one of the most profound religious upheavals in history

Getting away from it all

'Only quiet people live here, eating their sandwiches
Under the lilac while the boats go by.'

C H Sisson

Over the Wall: Berlin, May 1975

CITY PARKS

Freizeit Park, Tegel

On the edge of the Tegeler Forest, which covers more than 1,900ha (4,695 acres) of woodland, this is far and away Berlin's best out-of-town park. Attractions include an adventure playground, a paddling pool and trampolines; specially designated picnic and barbecue areas; table tennis, volley-ball and chess. There are rowing boats and paddle boats for hire near the marina and cycles can also be hired out. All facilities are clearly signposted, with times of opening, and each of the main areas is zoned off by trees and pathways. A short walk away is the Greenwich promenade, where the English theme extends to red telephone kiosks and post boxes. Private yachts ply the waters here, competing with the pleasure cruisers. The firm of Reederei Heinz Riedel advertises daily tours of the Tegeler See and Heiligen See, departing about every two hours. Shops and cafés are close at hand in the attractive suburb of Alt-Glienicke.
Boat to Greenwich Promenade or U-Bahn to Tegel.

Tiergarten

This famous park (*see pp96–7*), once a hunting ground for the Electors, is only a short distance away from the main sights around the Ku'damm (*see pp94–5*). Technically you are only allowed to sunbathe on the designated areas, but if in doubt follow the locals. A good stretch for lying out is in the vicinity of John-Foster-Dulles-Allee. Boats are available for hire near the Neuer See (the park's largest lake) and there's a café here, too. Adorning the route from Tiergarten S-Bahn station into the park and down towards the Landwehrkanal is an unusual collection of gas-lamps from many of the major cities of Europe. Also near the canal, and with a fine view of the Siegessäule (Victory Column), is the attractive Löwenbrücke (Lion's Bridge). Concerts take place in the summer in the secluded Parkhaus of the Englischer Garten, which begins north of Altonaer Strasse. Berlin Zoo is next door to the Tiergarten (entrance in Budapester Strasse). *U-Bahn or S-Bahn to Zoologischer Garten. S-Bahn to Tiergarten.*

Treptower Park

The central feature of this sprawling park, dating from 1876, is the massive Sowjetisches Ehrenmal (Soviet War Memorial) commemorating the 20,000 Soviet Red Army soldiers killed during the capture of Berlin in 1945.
S-Bahn to Treptower Park.

Viktoriapark

The park encompasses one of the highest points in Berlin (all of 66m/217ft), the Kreuzberg (Mountain of the Cross). A series of steep terraces leads majestically to a masterpiece by Karl Friedrich Schinkel, his Monument to the Wars of Liberation (1813–15). Constructed from iron, this is a graceful neo-Gothic structure, culminating in a delicate spire. Militant angels guard the niches, while a sequence of plaques commemorates the various battles of the war. The monument was completed in 1821 and is all that survives of Schinkel's intention to build an enormous cathedral in honour of the Liberation on Leipzigerplatz. There is a children's playground in the park and the Golgotha Café provides refreshment near the monument. Football teams from the local Turkish league play here on Sundays.
U-Bahn to Platz der Luftbrücke.

Volkspark Friedrichshain

This attractive park, looking rather out of place in a heavily industrial and neglected area, was landscaped by P J Lenné in the mid-19th century. It is ideally suited to picnics and ball games, but there is also an attractive rose garden and lake and a neo-Baroque fountain, the Märchenbrunnen (Fable Fountain), designed by Ignaz Taschner and featuring characters from German fairy tales.

Two artificial mounds, known as *Trümmerberge*, are composed of rubble from flak bunkers dating from World War II.

Also in the park (on the south side) is the Friedhof der Märzgefallenen, a cemetery commemorating those who died fighting in the abortive revolutions of 1848 and 1918. The statue of Lenin which once stood near the park has been removed.
Am Friedrichshain. Trams: 24 & 28.

Open spaces such as the Tiergarten are to be found everywhere in Berlin

GRUNEWALD

Its literal meaning is the 'green forest' and there can be no more apt description for this immense (32sq km/ 12sq miles) tract of scenic woodland, interspersed with dappled paths, lakes, secluded beaches, nature reserves and country inns. In the 16th century the Grunewald took the fancy of the Elector Joachim II, who stocked it with wild boar, deer and other quarry, and built a hunting lodge for himself and his guests.

After World War II, much of the forest, which consisted mainly of pine, was felled to provide fuel for the bombed-out population of Berlin; it was subsequently replaced with a more varied mixture of beech, birch, oak and ash. Slicing through the middle of the forest is the Avus, a race track completed in 1921 and turned into an autobahn extension in 1998.

Brücke-Museum

This modern art museum lies to the east of the Grunewaldsee, on Bussardsteig 9 (*see pp38–9*).

Chalet Suisse

This Swiss-style cottage serves meals and snacks. There is a children's playground and a garden cluttered with fanciful model animals and even a make-believe old carriage. The finishing touch is a lady in folk costume playing an organ.

Clayallee 99. Tel: (030) 832 6362. Open: daily 11.30am–midnight.

Grunewald – peace and quiet only half an hour's journey from the centre of Berlin

Grunewaldsee and around

Surrounded by woodland, peaceful except for the barking of dogs (Berlin claims to have more dogs than any other city in Europe), and teeming with wildlife, the Grunewaldsee is a gentle, 40-minute stroll from the main road. Just after Koenigsallee you will see signs for the Hundekehlefenn nature reserve (the general term for a nature reserve is *Naturschutzgebiet*). Follow the footpath down to the lake and its sandy beaches, which are ideal for swimming. (There is a nudist beach on the western side, marked FKK on maps.) Picnicking is also allowed here.

Just south of the lake is the Forsthaus Paulsborn, a smart but demure restaurant with an attractive terrace.

Grunewaldturm (Grunewald Tower)

This folly on the banks of the Havel was designed by the architect of the Kaiser William Memorial Church in 1897. The tower, which is 55m (180ft) high, affords panoramic views across the Havel and the surrounding forest.

Jagdschloss Grunewald

This is the hunting lodge built for the Elector Joachim II of Brandenburg in 1542. The outbuildings and stables were added later, beginning around 1700, and the original lodge was surrounded by a moat. The interior is decorated with paintings of hunting scenes, stuffed birds and stags' heads. Today the lodge is a museum, which includes a brief but pleasant tour. The Grosse Saal (Great Hall), with its magnificent wooden ceiling, is noteworthy because it is the only part of the original building to have survived. Most of the paintings were brought from other royal residences. Among the rather stiff portraits of the various Brandenburg rulers – and, somewhat incongruously, one of Julius Caesar by Rubens, acquired by the Great Elector – you will also find a Jordaens, a Bruegel, and several paintings by Cranach the Elder, including a languid Adam and Eve. Cross the grassed-over, cobbled courtyard to the barn, which has been converted into a hunting museum with all the paraphernalia of the chase. (Closed until early 2009 for restoration and maintenance.)

Hüttenweg 100. Tel: (331) 969 4202. Open: Apr–Sept 10am–6pm; Mar & Oct 10am–5pm; Nov–Feb 10am–4pm. Admission charge.

Krumme Lanke

A secluded lake suitable for swimming.

Langer Luchs

A marshy nature reserve, extending to the south of the Grunewaldsee.

Teufelsberg ('Devil's Mountain')

Despite appearances, this 115m (377ft) hill, lying north of the Grunewaldsee, is man-made. It was one of eight such mounds formed after World War II from the rubble cleared from Berlin's devastated buildings. Most of the work was done by women, who became known as *Trümmerfrauen*. *S-Bahn to Grunewald (Line 3). Bus: 115 to Pückler Strasse.*

Elector Joachim II's hunting lodge at Grunewald

MÜGGELSEE

Traditionally the lakeside resorts and forests around the Grosser Müggelsee were a favourite weekend and summer haunt of East Berliners. With unification, however, this still beautiful area was deprived of its captive market and now it has to compete with its Western rivals, Wannsee and Grunewald – no easy matter, as the location is still not as well known. However, there are several new hotels and restaurants to catch the tourist's eye. What is certain, however, is that the Müggelsee itself will always attract visitors. The placid waters stretch over some 750 hectares (1,853 acres), nearly three times the area of Wannsee, and the shores, with their reeds, water rushes, wildfowl, birds and wild flowers, are surprisingly unspoilt.

Friedrichshagen

This small, attractive town was founded in the 18th century by Frederick the Great as a settlement for cotton spinners. More than 100 Bohemian families were invited to colonise the area on condition that they took responsibility for planting mulberry trees for rearing silkworms. Friedrichshagen retains a village atmosphere, especially in the neighbourhood of Bölschestrasse, where some of the mulberry trees and original houses are still to be seen. Look out, too, for the 19th-century restaurant, Zum Maulbeerbaum, which has a reputation for traditional German cooking. Writers including Frank Wedekind, author of *Lulu* (later set to music by Alban Berg), and Gerhard Hauptmann found the atmosphere here congenial.

Not far away, along the Müggelseedamm, is the Wasserwerk Friedrichshagen, a neo-Gothic brick waterworks dating from the 1890s. It has now been converted to a museum illustrating the history of the Müggelsee in supplying Berlin with water. On the western fringes of the lake, at Fürstenwalder Damm, is an FKK (nudist beach).

S-Bahn line 3, two stops after Köpenick.

WILHELM VOIGT

The local folk-hero is Wilhelm Voigt, a mischievous shoemaker and petty criminal who one day in 1906 dressed up as a captain in the Prussian army, commandeered a squad of grenadiers in Plötzensee, then marched them to Köpenick. Without once thinking to question his orders, the soldiers entered the town hall, arrested the mayor and handed over the contents of the treasury to Voigt, who promptly vanished. Voigt is commemorated in the local summer festival and you'll see images of the 'captain' outside buildings and bars all around Köpenick.

Müggelseeperle

This sprawling holiday complex, a stone's throw along the lake from Rübezahl, offers accommodation as well as various restaurants and is now part of the Dorint hotel group. Ferries arrive at the pier here from Friedrichshagen before returning to Berlin via Treptow and Steglitz.

The Wasserwerk Friedrichshagen is now a waterworks museum

Rahnsdorf

The attraction here is the old fishing village, where fishermen's houses cluster around the lakeside, and the parish church.

S-Bahn line 3, one stop after Friedrichshagen, then bus 161 for 6 stops.

Rübezahl to the Teufelsee

The *Gaststätten* (restaurants) still have a certain charm of former GDR architecture, despite their almost complete restoration in recent years, and are well worth a visit. It's possible to pick up the ferry here, and cross the Müggelsee, but a more rewarding proposition might be to take the well-marked footpath to **Teufelsee**, the 'Devil's Lake', really little more than a pool surrounded by marsh and trees. Another footpath, marked *Wanderlehrpfad*, is a nature trail with indicators giving details of rocks, names of trees, birds, etc. The path leading to the Müggelberge (a mound rather than a hill) ends at the **Müggelturm**, a lookout tower with wonderful views of the lakes and woods. Restaurants and bars abound in the area.

Bus: 169 from Köpenick via Müggelheimer Damm.

WANNSEE

This stunning lakeside resort on the western fringes of Berlin offers every imaginable diversion – beaches, tennis, golf, watersports, river cruises, scenic walks and numerous places of interest.

Boat trips and excursions

The possibilities are endless. From Wannsee Bridge pier there are tours of Wannsee Island and excursions to Potsdam, Spandau, the Tegeler See and points around the Havel. Visitors with a BVG pass can take the ferry to Kladow – the most economical way to enjoy the magnificent views.

Blockhaus Nikolskoe

See pp30–31.
Bus: 216 from Wannsee station.

Kleist's grave

A plain granite stone strewn with flowers marks the site where the

The view of Wannsee from the Conference House

Romantic poet Heinrich von Kleist (*see p56*) committed suicide with his lover and companion, Henriette Vogel, on 21 November 1811. The inscription reads: 'Now, oh immortality, are you wholly mine'. The grave is situated in woodland overlooking the shores of Kleiner Wannsee, off Bismarck Strasse and very near the station.

Pfaueninsel

Peacock Island is an enjoyable, five-minute ferry ride from the opposite bank (small charge). It was acquired by Frederick William II in 1793 as a hideaway for himself and his mistress. However, premature death through the unlikely accident of being hit in the eye with a champagne cork cut short his enjoyment. It was his successor Frederick William III who turned the island into the idiosyncratic nature reserve it is today. It is an interesting place, for the terrain is populated not only by wildlife but also by numerous follies, the most prominent of which is a white-brick ruined castle, the Schloss, constructed in 1794–7.

The island is a special protection area, so there are no refreshments on sale and picnicking is confined to one designated area. But you are free to wander at leisure and enjoy a mock-Gothic farm with real geese, an entertaining bird reserve and, down by the pier, a miniature frigate presented by King George IV of England – and the peacocks, of course!

Schloss Glienicke

See pp55–7.
Bus: 116 from Wannsee station.

Strandbad Wannsee

Once glamorous and still popular with Berliners, this is the largest inland beach in Europe. Facilities include changing rooms, sun terraces, shops, eateries, slides, diving boards, a jetty, even life-sized chess. The entrance is well signposted from Nikolskoe station. *Admission charge.*

Wannsee Conference House

The mottled grey villa with beautiful views across the lake was once owned by a wealthy industrialist, Frederick Minoux. It was still known as the Villa Minoux in 1940 when it was acquired by the SS as a guesthouse. On 20 January 1942, the head of the Reich Central Security Office, Reinhard Heydrich, summoned leading SS officers and civil servants here to discuss the implementation of the policy of deportation and mass murder of up to 11 million European Jews. Ring the bell at the main gate for entry – owing to the attentions of neo-Nazis, the curators have had to adopt tight security measures.

The permanent exhibition is set out in 14 rooms and traces the whole horrifying story, from the origins of the Nazi dictatorship through the deportations, setting up of extermination camps and annihilation of the Jews to their belated deliverance

A glimpse of water at Müritz National Park

at the end of the war. Whole rooms are devoted to Auschwitz and the Warsaw Ghetto Uprising.

The focal point of the display is Room 6, where the conference itself took place. The conference minutes, which reveal an almost pedantic obsession with organisational niceties, were in the hand of Adolf Eichmann, who was eventually brought to justice by an Israeli court in 1962 and subsequently executed. An English-language leaflet is available at the information desk.

Am Grossen Wannsee 58. Tel: (030) 805 0110. www.ghwk.de. Open: daily 10am–6pm. Free admission. Bus: 114 from Wannsee station.

MÜRITZ NATIONAL PARK

To get away from it all, head north of Berlin for Germany's largest nature reserve. Its centrepiece, the Müritz National Park, was created in 1990 and extends over an area of more than 300sq km (116sq miles), from Waren in the north to Neustrelitz in the east and Wittstock, the source of the Havel, in the south. A place of extraordinary natural beauty, Müritz is easily accessible by car (take route E96 from Berlin), but on arrival it is much more rewarding to explore its riches on foot, taking any of the numerous and well-signposted pathways. The Müritzsee is only one of 117 lakes in the park, though stretching as it does for more than 27km (17 miles), it is the second-largest lake in Germany. In the winter this is an inhospitable landscape, bleak and windswept, the marshes shrouded in mist, hospitable terrain only for white-tailed eagles and black storks. In the summer, the lakes appear placid and benign – insects thrive among the breeding grounds of cranes and grey herons. Small oases of moorland and meadow support numerous varieties of rare grasses and wild flowers, orchids, and gentians among them, and numerous species of butterfly have been identified. White unhorned cattle and sheep graze here, too. Nearly two-thirds of the land consists of mixed forest, predominantly firs, alders and birches, which is the perfect habitat for wild deer.

While the pleasures of the National Park are inexhaustible, there is nothing to stop the visitor straying further afield, to the attractive towns of Neustrelitz and Wesenberg, for example – towns of Slav origin in a region which was first settled in Mesolithic times. When the naturalists depart, in come the archaeologists to discover the region's fascinating past. Recent finds include jewellery from the Bronze Age and Roman silverware.

Silver birch in the National Park

Shopping

Berlin is unrivalled as a Mecca for shopping. The Kurfürstendamm (Ku'damm), nearly 4km (2½ miles) long, is the main shopping street and visitors need not stray very far from here to find everything they need. Tired and hungry shoppers will be relieved to find that there are dozens of cafés, imbiss *stands and restaurants in the neighbourhood.*

The streets off the Ku'damm, especially Bleibtreustrasse and Pariser Strasse, are famous for fashion boutiques (not all the shops are exclusive, however). Antique shops (Berlin currently specialises in Art Deco) can be found in Goethestrasse, Pestalozzistrasse and Fasanenstrasse. The city's main department stores are also close at hand. Wertheim's is on the Ku'damm itself, across the road from the Europa-Center; KaDeWe (Kaufhaus des Westens) and Peek & Cloppenburg are around the corner of Wittenbergplatz. For an alternative to the Ku'damm, take the U-Bahn to Adenauerplatz and try the Wilmersdorferstrasse, a more compact and pedestrianised shopping area which offers a good range of shops, including several stores – Karstadt, for example.

Shopping on the east side

Since unification, Western-style shops have been opening all over former East Berlin, mainly boutiques and hi-tech stores. There is a wide range of shopping spots for fashionable clothing and shoes around U-Bahn Hackescher Markt. The Hackesche Höfe offers a vibrant young arts and gallery scene, entertainment, small shops, bars, cinemas and restaurants. Friedrichstrasse has major stores like Galeries Lafayette, Young Fashion, H&M and Benetton. The Galeries are just a part of the Friedrichstadt Passagen, consisting of Quartiers 205, 206 and 207, which are linked by a shopping passage. Prices in the newer stores are no more competitive than those in the West; however, private enterprise is also showing its face in the rapidly increasing numbers of market stalls which you'll find outside S-Bahn stations and along individual shopping streets in the remoter neighbourhoods. Clothing and other items here can be relatively cheap. It's certainly worth keeping an eye open for bargains.

Best buys

Souvenirs can be found in plentiful supply along the Ku'damm. T-shirts with Berlin emblems and logos are always a hit with teenagers and are not overly expensive. Shops at the museums sell notebooks, pens and other cheap items ideal for children to take back to friends. For the political tourist, chunks of concrete purporting to be pieces of the Berlin Wall are still on sale around Checkpoint Charlie and the Brandenburg Gate, at varying prices, depending on size. Don't kid yourself that you're buying the real thing, although you may just strike lucky; certainly don't pay more for a 'certificated' piece – the certificates are bogus. Eastern-bloc memorabilia is also readily available: everything from caps, belts and badges to greatcoats sporting the proper insignia and East German flags. All this paraphernalia is more likely to be authentic, having been sold off by departing or de-mobbed troops – but, again, you can never be sure. For a more upmarket meme
visit, shop for porcelain
KPM factory in Berlin o
expensive Meissen varie
for table linen, silverwa
Cameras are also a good buy, as are toys, for which the Germans are famous.

Bargains

The best place for bargains is the weekend market on Strasse des 17 Juni (*S-Bahn Tiergarten*) where you'll find a wide range of items, from books to fancy jewellery. A place for bits and pieces and real bargains is right in front of Rathaus Schöneberg, offering the most curious mixture of goods (and people as well) (*Schöneberg, John-F-Kennedy-Platz. Open: Sat–Sun 9am–4pm; U-Bahn to Innsbrucker Platz*).

Finally, for second-hand clothing it's worth a trek out to Garage in Nollendorf (*Ahornstrasse 2*), which is said to be Europe's biggest store of its kind.

The Hackesche Höfe centre on the east side of town

Shopping hours

Since 2006 Berlin has allowed privately owned stores to stay open 24 hours Monday to Friday (also 1pm to 8pm on the four Sundays before Advent). Many now follow this new policy. Most department stores and urban shopping centres open from 9am to 8pm Monday to Saturday.

VAT

Anyone buying more than €25 worth of goods from any one shop and intending to take them out of the European Union is entitled to a rebate on the VAT (*Mehrwertsteuer*). Simply fill out a form in the store, then, on leaving Germany, present it, along with the item and the receipt, to customs. Note that the rebate will be 6 to 11 per cent of the purchase price and not the full value of VAT.

Antiques

Berliner Antik & Flohmarkt

More than 60 dealers reside in the arches under the S-Bahn tracks. Fine antique furniture, jewellery, art and ceramics, mainly from the 1920s and 1930s.
S-Bahnbogen 190-203. Open: Wed–Sun 11am–6pm. U-Bahn or S-Bahn to Friedrichstrasse.

Suarezstrasse

Several antique shops, some specialising in Art Deco.
Charlottenburg, Suarezstrasse. S-Bahn to Charlottenburg.

Zille-Hof

Pots and pans, furniture, glasses, books, old clothes, bric-a-brac.
Fasanenstrasse 14. Tel: (030) 313 4333.

Books

Buchhandlung Heinrich Hugendubel

One of Berlin's biggest and best bookshops, with an upstairs café.
Tauentzienstrasse 13. Tel: (030) 214 060.

Kiepert

All subjects. Good on travel.
Hardenbergstrasse 9a. Tel: (030) 318 0523.

Marga Schöller

The best shop for books in English, and for German-language books on Berlin.
Knesebeckstrasse 33–34. Tel: (030) 881 1112.

Chocolates

Leysieffer

Berlin's epicurean chocolatier since 1909; fancy-wrapped gift boxes sold here. Also on site, up the stairs: an old-fashioned, balconied bakery café for *Kaffee und Kuchen.*
Kurfüstendamm 218. Tel: (030) 885 7480.

Clothes

Claudia Skoda

Ready-to-wear and custom-fitted women's wear by one of the city's hottest fashion designers.
Alte Schönhauser Strasse 35. Tel: (030) 280 7211.

H&M

Swedish clothes chain, cheap and up-to-date.
Kurfürstendamm 20–24. Tel: (030) 882 5239.

Mientus

The latest styles in casual and formal clothing for men; very 'in' and positively pricey.
Wilmersdorfer Strasse 73. Tel: (030) 323 9077.

Molotow
Clothes by Berlin designers at average to expensive prices.
Gneisenaustrasse 112.
Tel: (030) 693 0818.

Department stores

KaDeWe
Tauentzienstrasse 21–4.
Tel: (030) 21210.
Karstadt
Wilmersdorferstrasse 118.
Tel: (030) 311 050.
Wertheim
Kurfürstendamm 231.
Tel: (030) 880 030.

Jewellery

Kaufhaus Schrill
Fun jewellery, costumes, wigs and accessories.
Bleibtreustrasse 46.
Tel: (030) 882 4048.
Open: Mon–Fri noon–7pm, Sat 11am–4pm.
Rio
Smart and sophisticated, with prices to match.
Bleibtreustrasse 52.
Tel: (030) 313 3152.

Markets

Strasse des 17 Juni
Ideal for picking up gifts, especially embroidery, lace, ethnic jewellery and artwork – everything, in fact.
Tel: (030) 322 8199.
Open: weekends.
Winterfeldmarkt
Where Berliners shop. Ideal for whiling away a Saturday morning, with plenty of cafés.
Winterfeldplatz, Schöneberg.
Open: Wed & Sat 8am–1pm.

Perfume

Harry Lehmann
A family business where you can even bring your own bottle to be filled.
Kantstrasse 106.
Tel: (030) 324 3582.

Porcelain

KPM
Pottery manufactured by the famous Royal Porcelain Factory, founded in the 18th century by Frederick the Great.
Kurfürstendamm 26a.
Tel: (030) 88672 113.
Unter den Linden 35.
Tel: (030) 206 4150.

Sport

Karstadt Sport
Everything for the sporting man and woman.
Joachimstaler Strasse 5–6.

Toys

Berline
An ama
handm
Knesebe
Tel: (030) 315 70077.
Steiff Boutique
Some of the most gorgeous stuffed animals in all kinds of shapes, colours and sizes can be found here. Shop sells children's clothes too.
Kurfürstendamm 220.
Tel: (030) 887 21919.

A street stall selling East German souvenirs

Film

Berlin's love affair with the silver screen began in 1895, when the brothers Max and Emil Skladanowsky showed a primitive film at the Wintergarten using the world's first projector, the bioscope. The first cinema arrived just four years later in an otherwise anonymous building on Münzstrasse.

During World War I, the propaganda needs of the army gave birth to a German film industry whose financing was masterminded by the Chief of Staff, General Erich Ludendorff. UFA (Universum Film Aktiengesellschaft) began making patriotic features in purpose-built studios in Babelsberg near Potsdam. Films were also made in Schöneberg. The heyday of UFA came in the 1920s with a succession of classic films, including *Dr Caligari*, the futuristic fantasy *Metropolis* – a spectacular flop at the box office – and *The Blue Angel*, which became the vehicle for a rising young starlet, Marlene Dietrich.

Under the Nazis, UFA became the tool and plaything of Hitler's propaganda chief, Joseph Goebbels. Goebbels used the casting couch to get his way with beautiful young hopefuls, while hiring big names like Werner Krauss to star in unashamedly anti-Semitic films. Meanwhile, the actress-turned-filmmaker Leni Riefenstahl was making her two classic propaganda pageants for Hitler, *Der Triumph des Willens* (*Triumph of the Will*), a cine-montage of the 1934 Nuremberg party rally, and *Olympia*, eulogising the Berlin Olympic Games of 1936. Hitler himself was never portrayed on screen except as the model Prussian, Frederick the Great. But to win the hearts and minds of German cinema audiences it was necessary to resort to pure, unadulterated entertainment. During the dark days of the war, escapist Hollywood-style fantasies soothed the nerves of a gloomy and apprehensive population.

In recent years, Berlin itself has been the star of a number of films, including Wim Wenders' *Wings of Desire* and Rainer Werner Fassbinder's epic *Berlin Alexanderplatz*, the longest commercially released film on record at 15 hours 21 minutes. Many of Germany's most original post-war film directors, including Wenders and Fassbinder, trained at UFA before going on to make their careers elsewhere.

Film remains something of an obsession with Berliners, and the city's international film festival, held in February, is second in importance only to the Venice Biennale.

The modernist architecture of Kino International, one of Berlin's many cinemas

Entertainment

Berlin thrives on an embarrassment of cultural riches and the range could not be more eclectic – from Grand Opera to Phantom of the Opera, *from symphony concerts to rock concerts. There's contemporary and classical dance, theatre of every conceivable variety, a feast of film, and discos and nightclubs for those with the necessary stamina. The fun extends from dusk to dawn, for Berlin is a city that never sleeps.*

Ticket agencies

Berlin Ticket im KaDeWe
Tauentzienstrasse. Tel: (030) 217 7754.
Hekticket
Last-minute tickets.
Hardenbergstrasse 29d & Alexanderplatz. Tel: (030) 230 9930. For additional information, visit www.berlin-info.de
Kant-Kasse
Krummestrasse 55. Tel: (030) 313 4554.

Listings magazines

The *ExBerliner* in English provides information about art, culture, entertainment and nightlife in Berlin, and is available free in cafés, hotels, pubs, shops and cinemas. *Tip* and *Zitty* appear twice monthly – comprehensive but unwieldy, and in German; *Berlin Programm,* a monthly, is also in German but more manageable.

THEATRE

The golden age of the Berlin theatres was the 1920s and 1930s, when the dominating figures included the playwrights Bertolt Brecht and Carl Zuckmayer, the great director Max Reinhardt, and superb actresses such as Lotte Lenya and Elisabeth Bergner. Currently the theatres are in crisis, as the Senate tries to reduce the huge budget deficit. There are few productions in English.

Berliner Ensemble
Brecht's famous theatre, specialising in his plays and others in the radical tradition.
Am Bertolt-Brecht-Platz.
Tel: (030) 284 08155.
U-Bahn or S-Bahn to Friedrichstrasse.
Deutsches Theater
Max Reinhardt directed here; classical repertoire.
Schumannstrasse 13. Tel: (030) 284 41225.
U-Bahn or S-Bahn to Friedrichstrasse.
Schaubühne am Lehniner Platz
A well-deserved reputation for innovative and experimental modern drama.

Kurfürstendamm 153. Tel: (030) 890 023. U-Bahn to Adenauerplatz.

Theater des Westens

Broadway shows, musicals.

Kantstrasse 12. Tel: (030) 882 2888. U-Bahn or S-Bahn to Zoologischer Garten.

CABARET AND VARIETY

Anyone hoping to catch a glimpse of cabaret as it was in the Berlin of the 1920s is liable to be disappointed, although attempts to revive the earlier variety-music hall tradition, with circus acts, have fared somewhat better. Political satire is still very much part of the Berlin cabaret scene, but, needless to say, you'll need excellent German to appreciate all the nuances – or even to get the point at all. If you think you fit the bill, consult the listings magazines – the choice is limitless.

Bar jeder Vernunft

A tent with velvet loges, mirrors and candlelight, showing special *chanson*, cabaret, comedy and revue programmes, some in English.

Tiergarten, Schaperstrasse 26. Tel: (030) 883 1582. U-Bahn to Spichernstrasse or Kurfürstendamm.

BKA–Berliner Kabarett Anstalt

Alternative cabaret in Kreuzberg, popular with Berliners.

Mehringdamm 32–34. Tel: (030) 251 0112.

U-Bahn to Mehringdamm.

Chamäleon Varieté

Combines old variety tradition with modern style. Located in a restored *Jugendstil* ambience.

Mitte, Rosenthaler Strasse 40/Hackesche Höfe. Tel: (030) 282 7118.

S-Bahn to Hackescher Markt.

A pleasant view of the Deutsches Theater

Chez Nous

Transvestite show.

Marburger Strasse 14. Tel: (030) 213 1810. U-Bahn to Kurfürstendamm or Wittenbergplatz.

Die Distel

Formerly the scourge of the GDR establishment, now casting a satirical eye over unified Germany in the circa-1911 Admiralspalast.

Friedrichstrasse 101. Tel: (030) 204 4704. U-Bahn or S-Bahn to Friedrichstrasse.

Friedrichstadtpalast

Glitzy floor show with music, dance, circus acts, etc.

Friedrichstrasse 107. Tel: (030) 23262 326; www.friedrichstadtpalast.de. U-Bahn or S-Bahn to Friedrichstrasse.

Wintergarten

Following on an old variety tradition.

Potsdamer Strasse 96.
Tel: (030) 250 08888.
U-Bahn to Kurfürstenstrasse.

Alternative events

UFA-Fabrik

The place to visit for alternative events of all kinds – be it music, theatre, film or dance.

Kreuzberg, Viktoriastrasse 10–18. Tel: (030) 755 030. www.ufafabrik.de. U-Bahn to Ullsteinstrasse.

MUSIC

Berlin has an enviable musical tradition that goes back to 1791 and the founding of the Singakademie. The young composer Felix Mendelssohn led the rediscovery of the music of J S Bach with a performance of the *St Matthew Passion* in the 1840s. Later in the century Liszt, Berlioz and Wagner all appeared in Berlin, but the city is most famous for the Berlin Philharmonic Orchestra, founded in 1882 and still gracing the city today.

The façade of the neoclassical Deutsche Staatsoper on Unter den Linden

Jazz/folk

Irish Inn
Folk and Guinness® from boisterous Celts.
Damaschkestrasse 28. Tel: (030) 324 4371. U-Bahn to Adenauerplatz. S-Bahn to Charlottenburg.

Kalkscheune
Various artists and bands.
Mitte, Johannisstrasse 2. Tel: (030) 590 0434. U-Bahn or S-Bahn to Friedrichstrasse.

Quasimodo
For jazz lovers with eclectic tastes.
Kantstrasse 12a. Tel: (030) 312 8086. www.quasimodo.de. U-Bahn to Zoologischer Garten.

A Trane Jazzclub (swank jazz club)
Charlottenburg, Bleibtreustrasse 1. Tel: (030) 313 2550. U-Bahn to Uhlandstrasse or S-Bahn to Savignyplatz.

Opera/ballet

Deutsche Oper Berlin
A great opera tradition, despite the artless modern venue – also modern ballet.
Charlottenburg, Bismarckstrasse 35. Tel: (030) 343 8401. U-Bahn to Deutsche Oper.

Deutsche Staatsoper
Classical opera and ballet in a classical setting, the opera directed by eminent conductor and pianist Daniel Barenboim.
Unter den Linden 7. Tel: (030) 203 54555. U-Bahn and S-Bahn to Friedrichstrasse. Bus: 101.

Komische Oper
Operettas and ballet.
Behrenstrasse 55–57. Tel: (030) 479 974. U-Bahn to Französische Strasse. Bus: 100.

Rock/pop

Deutschlandhalle
Popular venue for rock concerts.
Messedamm 26. Tel: (030) 303 84223. S-Bahn to Westkreuz.

ICC Berlin (International Congress Centre)
Often used for pop concerts.
Messedamm 26. Tel: (030) 30380. U-Bahn to Kaiserdamm. S-Bahn to Westkreuz. Buses: 104, 105, 110, 149 & 219.

Waldbühne
Germany's largest open-air arena: 22,000-seat amphitheatre for summer concerts – rock bands perform here, as well as opera stars like Placido Domingo.
Glockenturmstrasse/Passenheimer Strasse 1/19. Tel: (030) 304 0676.

Symphony/chamber concerts

Kammermusiksaal
Part of the Philharmonie complex, this smaller hall is used for chamber concerts.
Herbert-von-Karajan-Strasse 1. Tel: (030) 254 880. S-Bahn to Potsdamer Platz. Buses: 129, 148, 248 & 348.

Konzerthaus
Home of the Berlin Symphony Orchestra, though other orchestras play here too.
Gendarmenmarkt 2. Tel: (030) 203 0921. U-Bahn Französische Strasse or Hausvogteiplatz.

(Cont. on p154)

Cabarets and revues

A nightclub in Nollendorfplatz

'Life is a cabaret' declares Sally Bowles in Bob Fosse's 1972 film. And for some, life in 1920s Berlin was, indeed, one long round of parties, champagne, jazz music and every conceivable kind of hedonistic pleasure. Certainly Berlin lived up to its reputation as a Mecca of vice, Sodom and Gomorrah rolled into one. Decadent and dangerous, Berlin invited its children to 'Take a walk on the wild side'. Every imaginable sexual taste was catered for. For homosexuals there were the Kleistkasino and the clubs around Nollendorfplatz – still the centre of the gay scene today. Lesbians, attired in dinner jackets and monocles, headed for the Mali club, while the transvestites' favourite haunt was the Eldorado.

Those with more conventional tastes were not disappointed either. At the Apollo Theatre on Friedrichstrasse, scantily clad girls posed in sacrilegious imitation of the goddess of peace and her acolytes on top of the Brandenburg Gate. For the less artistically minded there were the dance troops – the Tiller girls at the Scala, for example. Alternatively, one could go to the Resi (Residenzcasino) on Alexanderplatz, where each table was provided with a telephone for flirting with fellow diners.

But conspicuous wealth and loose living was not the whole story. Liza Minnelli's portrayal of Sally Bowles may be an artistic *tour de force*, but it was not true to life. The real Sally was a struggling English cabaret singer called Jean Ross, who appeared in the seediest nightclubs while sharing the 'life of the unemployed' with the writer Christopher Isherwood and his friends W H Auden and Stephen Spender. At least Marlene Dietrich's performance in *The Blue Angel* was drawn from experience. She was in the back row of the chorus line of a revue on the Ku'damm when she was talent-spotted by an associate of the director Joseph von Sternberg. The film made her career and she was soon off to Hollywood.

Since 1989 a concerted effort has been made to revive the old cabaret tradition, albeit shorn of sexual and other excesses. Perhaps it is all rather tame by comparison with the 1920s, but there is plenty of variety: women impersonators, glitzy showgirls, circus acts and political satire.

Liza Minnelli as Sally Bowles in the film *Cabaret*

Philharmonie

Scharoun's masterpiece, this wonderful auditorium is the home of the world-famous Berlin Philharmonic.
Herbert-von-Karajan-Strasse 1. Tel: (030) 254 88132. S-Bahn to Potsdamer Platz. Buses: 129, 148, 248 & 348.

Other music venues

Tempodrom

This architecturally stunning music hall, shaped like a tent, near the ruins of the former grand station Anhalter Bahnhof, hosts all kinds of live music, including pop and jazz.
Kreuzberg, Möckernstrasse 10–25. Tel: (030) 695 33885. U-Bahn to Anhalter Bahnhof.

CINEMA

Berlin became the capital of Germany's cinema industry in the early 1920s with the founding of the UFA studios in Babelsberg. The Berlin Film Festival, held in February, is the time to see the best in international films. All films are dubbed unless indicated by OF (films in the original without subtitles) or OmU (original soundtrack with German subtitles). The following cinemas show films in English:

Arsenal

Tiergarten, Potsdamer Strasse 2. Tel: (03) 269 55100. U-Bahn or S-Bahn to Potsdamer Platz.

Babylon

Dresdner Strasse 126. Tel: (030) 616 09693. U-Bahn to Kottbusser Tor.

Summer nights in Berlin, all the fun of the fair

CinemaxX Potsdamer Platz

Tiergarten, Voxstrasse 2. Tel: (030) 443 16316. U-Bahn or S-Bahn to Potsdamer Platz.

Delphi

Kantstrasse 12a. Tel: (030) 312 1026. U-Bahn or S-Bahn to Zoologischer Garten.

Odeon

Hauptstrasse 116. Tel: (030) 787 04019. U-Bahn to Kleistpark or Innsbrucker Platz.

Schaubühne

Charlottenburg, Kurfürstendamm 153. Tel: (03) 089 0023. U-Bahn to Adenauerplatz.

NIGHTCLUBS/DISCOS

The scene, like everywhere else, is constantly changing. Refreshingly, most clubs charge only a small entry fee or none at all, though drink prices are predictably steep. Discos and clubs stay open late or very late. The following is necessarily a tiny selection: if you prefer to go on spec and take pot luck, wander around the Ku'damm at midnight. Kreuzberg has an excellent late-night scene – for nightclubs try Oranienstrasse.

Bierhimmel

Cool café for youngsters.

Kreuzberg, Oranienstrasse 183. Tel: (030) 615 3122. U-Bahn to Kottbusser Tor.

Big Eden

Living on past glories, very loud, very crowded but lively. For the very young!

Kurfürstendamm 202. Tel: (030) 882 6120. U-Bahn to Uhlandstrasse.

Café Keese

Fun for ageing ravers. Strict dress code – collar and tie for gents. Live band.

Bismarckstrasse 108. Tel: (030) 312 9111. U-Bahn to Ernst-Reuter-Platz.

Knaack Klub

In business since 1952, a Prenzlauer Berg nightlife hangout for high-decibel music, from live techno bands to karaoke.

Greifswalder Strasse 224. Tel: (030) 442 7060. Open: 8pm–late. U-Bahn to Eberswalder Strasse.

Metropol

Very popular weekend venue with Berliners, in a famous Art Deco theatre.

Nollendorfplatz 5. Tel: (030) 216 4122. U-Bahn to Nollendorfplatz.

Oxymoron

Nice clubby atmosphere, funk disco on special days.

Hackesche Höfe, Rosenthaler Strasse 40–41. Tel: (030) 283 91886. S-Bahn to Hackescher Markt.

Sage Club

The hottest club, house and funk, Sage Club is a must for hipsters; posh interior décor.

Mitte, Heinrich Heine Strasse/ Köpenicker Strasse. Tel: (030) 278 7694. U-Bahn to Heinrich Heine Strasse.

CASINO

Spielbank Berlin

Tiergarten, Marlene-Dietrich-Platz. Tel: (030) 255 990. U-Bahn or S-Bahn to Potsdamer Platz.

The Schaubühne cinema on Kurfürstendamm

GALLERIES AND EXHIBITIONS

One of the first business ventures to revive after the end of World War II was the commercial art market. Today there are around 150 galleries in Berlin dealing in paintings, sculptures, ceramics, posters, graphics and photographs. The auction houses Christie's and Sotheby's also have branches in the city. There are two distinct areas, geographically and commercially. The galleries in the streets off the Ku'damm, particularly Fasanenstrasse, Knesebeckstrasse and Wielandstrasse, specialise in the work of established contemporary artists and in the art of the late 19th and early 20th centuries. The old working-class suburbs of Kreuzberg, Scheunenviertel and Prenzlauer Berg are home to galleries featuring up-and-coming artists, as well as those who have chosen to reject the commercial market entirely in favour of cooperative ventures.

Visiting the galleries around the Ku'damm does not entail spending vast sums of money – the entertainment lies in seeing just what is on offer. It is worth bearing in mind, for example, that one is more likely to come across artists from the German Expressionist movement and the Neue Sachlichkeit (New Objectivity), names like Dix, Kirchner, Heckel and Liebermann, in the auction rooms of Fasanenstrasse than in the city's public galleries. The sale rooms of the Villa Grisebach regularly turn up work by the famous German Romantic artist Menzel, as well as Klee and Nolde, while the equally famous Brusberg Gallery might be exhibiting artists of the stature of Dalí, Max Ernst and even Picasso. The ambience of these galleries is in itself relaxing and enjoyable – there is a cultivated atmosphere in the 19th-century drawing rooms of the *Jugendstil* villas of Fasanenstrasse, architectural monuments in their own right. And some galleries, such as the Bremer, even have an evening bar scene where it is possible to see the market at work.

Kreuzberg and the other districts mentioned earlier offer a completely different experience. Here, little-known but talented artists exhibit their work in *ateliers* carved out of old bakeries, warehouses and factories, and the exhibitions, invariably informal, are often accompanied by various kinds of 'happenings' involving anything from music to mime. Prenzlauer Berg, formerly in East Germany, was a centre of political radicalism and alternative culture, and the artists here are now anxiously coming to terms with the implications of reunification. The best way of exploring the alternative scene is simply to wander the streets. Try Curvystrasse in Kreuzberg, the Hackesche Höfe near Oranienburger Strasse in the Scheunenviertel, and Tucholskystrasse and Auguststrasse in Mitte.

Berlin Programm has a special section devoted to galleries, giving up-to-date information on current exhibitions.

Around the Ku'damm

Galerie Bremer

Specialises in established modern German artists.

Fasanenstrasse 37. Tel: (030) 881 4908. Open: Tue–Fri 2–6pm, Sat 11am–1pm. U-Bahn to Uhlandstrasse.

Galerie Brusberg

Contemporary painting and sculpture occasionally featuring 20th-century masters like Picasso and Miró.

Kurfürstendamm 213. Tel: (030) 882 7682. Open: Tue–Fri 10am–6.30pm, Sat 10am–2pm. U-Bahn to Uhlandstrasse.

Galerie Fahnemann

For anyone interested in Pop Art.

Gipsstrasse 14. Tel: (030) 883 9897. Open: Tue–Fri 1–6.30pm, Sat 11am–2pm. U-Bahn to Weinmeisterstrasse.

Galerie Pels-Leusden (Villa Grisebach)

Next to the Käthe-Kollwitz-Museum, specialising in art from the 19th and 20th centuries, especially German.

Villa Grisebach, Fasanenstrasse 25. Tel: (030) 885 9
10am–6.30pm, S
to Uhlandstrasse.

Other areas

Galerie am Prate

Contemporary ar
and photography.

Prenzlauer Berg, Kastanienallee 7–9. Tel: (030) 440 38366. Open: Tue–Sun 3–9pm. U-Bahn to Eberswalder Strasse.

Galerie Wohnmaschine

Tucholskystrasse 35. Tel: (030) 308 72015. www.wohnmaschine.de. Open: Tue, Wed, Fri & Sat 2–7pm, Thur 5–9pm. S-Bahn to Oranienburger Strasse.

Hackesche Höfe

The artists' studios are dotted about the restored warehouses, and visitors are welcome.

Mitte, Rosenthaler Strasse. S-Bahn to Hackescher Markt.

Mora Café-Galerie

Kreuzberg, Grossbeerenstrasse 57a. Tel: (030) 785 0585. Open: daily 11am–1am. U-Bahn to Mehringdamm.

The Kreuzberg district has art all around, here on a hotel façade

Children

Berlin has no shortage of attractions for children, especially among its huge assortment of museums. For outdoor fun, the Tiergarten, the Zoo and Legoland are all in the centre and, not far away, there are plenty of forests and lakes to enjoy. Also, a trip down the River Spree is always an option when children tire of walking.

Boat trips

There are boat stops at regular intervals along the Spree so one can act on impulse. *See pp114–15.*

General sports facilities

The Sport und Erholungszentrum (SEZ) in Landsberger Allee is unbeatable but probably best suited to older children. There is a roller-skating centre in the Hasenheide (U-Bahn to Hermannplatz), where you can hire skates.

Legoland Discovery Centre

New interactive family attraction at Potsdamer Platz comprising a 4-D cinema, play area, food court and featuring scale-model Miniland Berlin, with major city landmarks made of multicoloured LEGO bricks.
Mitte, Sony Center.
Tel: (030) 301 0400.
Open: Mon–Fri 10am–5pm, Sat–Sun 10am–6pm. Admission charge.
U-Bahn to Potsdamer Platz.

Museums

The **Museum für Naturkunde** has a gigantic dinosaur skeleton to marvel at, as well as other attractions. The Ethnologisches Museum (Ethnography Museum – *see p43*) has a rich and stimulating collection of exhibits, including masks, canoes, reconstructed dwellings and weapons. If you are visiting the Dahlem Museums there is a section specially designed for children. Older children will appreciate the Haus am Checkpoint Charlie (*see p58*), an entertaining account of the history of the Wall with an emphasis on escapology. Another favourite is the Deutsches Technikmuseum (German Museum of Technology, *see pp48–9*), with its collections of vintage cars, aeroplanes and steam trains.
Museum für Naturkunde,
Invalidenstrasse 43. Tel: (030) 209 38591.
Open: Tue–Fri 9.30am–5pm,
Sat–Sun 10am–6pm.
www.museum.hu.berlin.de.
U-Bahn or S-Bahn to Friedrichstrasse.

Out of town

There are acres of woodland around Berlin where children can romp and let off steam. Wannsee (S-Bahn to Nikolassee) and Müggelsee (S-Bahn to Friedrichshagen or Rahnsdorf) both have beaches; or there are the lakeside beaches in Grunewald – ideal for picnics and with nature trails to hand. Also in Grunewald is the Chalet Suisse, with its novelty garden. While in Wannsee, visit Peacock Island, where the animals and follies will keep children amused.

Parks

Freizeit Park, Tegel (*see p132*), offers enough for children to do for at least half a day, and there is the additional possibility of boat rides.

Playgrounds

There is no shortage of playgrounds in Berlin. Try Ludwigkirchplatz (off the Ku'damm), Käthe Kollwitz Platz in the Tiergarten or Monbijou Park, near Museum Island.

Swimming pools

There is Kinderschwimmbad am Monbijou-Platz (entrance on Oranienburger Strasse) just by Museum Island or **Blub Badeparadies** which has fountains, waterfalls, wave pool and a 120m- (394ft-) long 'superslide'.

Buschkrugallee 64. Tel: (030) 609 060. Open: Mon–Fri 10am–11pm, Sat–Sun 9am–midnight. U-Bahn to Grenzallee.

Zoos

Naturally Berlin has two! The Berlin **Zoologischer Garten** was founded in the 1840s, but much of the stock was wiped out by wartime bombing. The Aquarium, next door (separate entry fee), is by far the most interesting part. An attractive alternative is the **Tierpark**.

Zoologischer Garten, Budapester Strasse 26. Tel: (030) 254 010. Open: daily 9am–6.30pm. U-Bahn or S-Bahn to Zoologischer Garten.

Tierpark, Am Tierpark 125, Friedrichsfelde. Tel: (030) 515 310. Open: daily 9am–dusk. U-Bahn to Tierpark (line 6).

Sea Life Centre

Aquarium populated with 2,500 creatures (including sharks and manta rays) from German waters, swimming round in a ceiling-high cylindrical tank called the Aquadom.

Mitte, Spandauer Strasse 3. Tel: (030) 992 800. Open: daily 10am–7pm. Admission charge. U-Bahn to Alexanderplatz or S-Bahn to Hackescher Markt.

Other attractions

The circus regularly comes to town, as do fairgrounds. Consult *Berlin Programm* or *Tourist Information* for current details. Puppet theatres, while uniformly in German, are accessible enough, especially to the very young.

Grips Theatre

A favourite with German parents.

Altonaer Strasse 22. Tel: (030) 397 4747. S-Bahn to Bellevue.

Sport and leisure

Berliners take their sport seriously. In fact, the number of Berliners participating in sport is said to be on the increase, following a high-profile campaign by the local sports federation.

Sports facilities are well up to the mark and most needs are catered for. Those wishing to take gentle exercise will find a surfeit of beautiful places in which to go jogging, to walk or to take a swim. As for spectator sports, ice hockey remains a favourite here, while basketball and American football are beginning to catch on. Berlin is not, however, renowned for its soccer, an embarrassing shortcoming given Germany's outstanding record in the sport.

The best source of information for visitors is *Berlin Programm*, which includes a monthly sporting calendar with full details of addresses, telephones, etc.

Another useful contact address is Landessportbund Berlin, Jesse-Owens-Allee 1–2. *Tel: (030) 300 020.*

The best overall sports facility is the **Sport und Erholungszentrum (SEZ)** at Landsberger Allee 77 (*tel: (030) 42283 320*), where facilities include a swimming pool, gym, skating rink, bowling alley, and volleyball and badminton courts. The Berlin Marathon in October is one of the main sport events in town.

Billiards

Billiard Palace

Popular with local enthusiasts.
Uhlandstrasse 188. Tel: (030) 313 4819. U-Bahn to Uhlandstrasse.

Boating

Rowing boats are available for hire on any number of Berlin lakes – such as the Freizeitpark Tegel, Tiergarten (Neuer See) and Strandbad Wannsee.

Bowling

Bowling am Kurfürstendamm

The most central venue.
Kurfürstendamm 156. Tel: (030) 882 5030. U-Bahn to Adenauerplatz.

Cycling

Bicycle hire from: **Fahrradstation**
Friedrichstrasse 95. Tel: (030) 283 84848. Open: Mon–Fri 8am–4pm, Sat & Sun

10am–4pm. U-Bahn or S-Bahn to Friedrichstrasse. Hackescher Höfe, Hof 7. Tel: (030) 283 84848. Open: Mon–Fri 10am–7pm, Sat 10am–3pm. Closed: Sun. Also try **Grunewald S-Bahn station** during the summer. The most detailed map for cyclists is *ADFC-Radtourenkarte.*

Fishing

For information on where to fish and how to obtain the necessary licence, contact:

Fischereiamt beim Senator für Stadtentwicklung und Umweltschutz
Havelchaussee 149. Tel: (030) 305 2047.

Football

Berlin's national Bundesliga teams are Hertha BSC (first division) and FC Union (second division). For further information contact:

Berliner Fussball-Verband
Tel: (030) 891 11047.

Horse racing

Trabrennbahn Karlshorst
Trabrennbahn Karlshorst. Tel: (030) 500 1710. Treskowallee 129 (trot races).

Galopprennbahn Hoppegarten
Goetheallee 1 (03342) 38930 (gallop races).

Ice skating

There are rinks at the Eisstadion. *Fritz-Wildung-Strasse. Tel: (030) 823 4060. S-Bahn to Hohenzollerndamm.*

Riding

Berlin's main riding school is **Equestrian Sports Park.** *Treskowallee 129, Lichtenberg. Tel: (030) 500 17121.*

Roller skating

Inline-Skating Halle
Franklinstrasse 5–7. Tel: (030) 314 27810.

Running

The Berlin Marathon is held annually on the last Sunday in September or the first Sunday in October.

The Tiergarten is a popular venue for joggers.

Swimming

Indoor swimming at:

Blub Badeparadies
Buschkrugallee 64. Tel: (030) 609 060.
There is also the **Olympia-Schwimmstadion** at Olympischer Platz. Outdoor swimming is available around many of the inland lakes and at **Strandbad Wannsee** (*tel: (030) 803 5450*).

Tennis/squash

Courts can be hired by the hour at **Preusseu-Park Tennis and Squash.** *Kamenzer Damm 34. Tel: (030) 775 1051.*

Football is a popular sport in Germany – in 2006 it hosted the World Cup

Food and drink

In common with most of Central Europe, traditional German cuisine places the main emphasis on meat, especially pork, though the ubiquitous sausage is not de rigueur. *Potatoes are the second chief ingredient, served up with pickled cabbage (*Sauerkraut*), beans, onions and peas. Portions are huge, and if by any chance you have room left for dessert, then the* Torten *and pastries represent a formidable challenge. Calorie-counting, needless to say, has no place in the traditional German kitchen.*

Berlin cooking conforms largely to the German pattern. The local taste for salty food goes back to the time of Frederick the Great and the salt monopoly. Berliners also have traditionally always been great fans of the potato.

Local specialities include *Buletten* (meatballs, introduced by the Huguenot community in the 17th century); *Aal grün* (eel served in a dill or parsley sauce), eel being in plentiful supply in the local rivers; and *Kartoffelpuffer* (the Berlin version of the savoury potato pancake). During the last 30 years, however, there has been a revolution in the eating habits of the Berliner, thanks partly to the raising of health consciousness, but mainly to the influence of the immigrant communities from Yugoslavia, Italy, Turkey and the Middle East.

Nowadays young Berliners would rather opt for a pizza than a plateful of roast pork. 'New German Cuisine', which originated in the south, is also the rage, especially with the prosperous yuppie types. This places a firm emphasis on quality rather than quantity (many will find the portions mean), and on presentation. Standards are generally high, but so are prices – too much so, in the opinion of many locals.

Tradition has been preserved in one respect, however: the Berliner still favours a large and varied breakfast, typically consisting of bread rolls and several kinds of sausage and eggs, and you will find numerous cafés serving breakfast more or less throughout the day. This practice (theoretically) does away with the need for lunch, and the increasing trend is for the main meal to be taken in the evening.

TYPICAL DISHES AND SPECIALITIES

Soups and snacks

Bulette a cross between a hamburger and an extra-size meatball.

Currywurst pork sausage slathered with curry-laced ketchup.
Hackepeter a kind of rissole.
Kartoffelsuppe potato soup with bacon.
Leberknödelsuppe dumpling soup with liver, onions, garlic.
Linsensuppe lentil soup, often containing sausage.
Soleier pickled eggs.

Main courses

Berliner Schlachteplatte liver sausage and boiled pork.
Eisbein pickled knuckle of pork, traditionally served with mashed potatoes and *Sauerkraut.*
Kartoffelpuffer a Berlin variant of fried potato cake.
Kasseler pickled pork chops, served with red cabbage.
Pellkartoffeln mit Quark jacket potatoes with curd cheese – and linseed oil if you want it!

Fish

Brathering grilled herring.
Matjeshering raw herring fillets served with onion, apple and gherkins in cream.

Dessert

Baumkuchen 'tree cake', made with potato flour, almonds and apricot jam.

Intimate dining atmosphere at Rocco restaurant

Where to eat

In terms of sheer variety, Berlin, with its hundreds of restaurants offering every conceivable cuisine from around the world, is one of the best cities for eating out in the whole of Europe. Restaurants are concentrated on the west side, especially on the Ku'damm, in the streets off Savigny Platz, and around Hardenbergstrasse, but you will find them everywhere – so if you see a place that takes your fancy, note it down.

The best place for Turkish food is Kreuzberg, especially the streets near Kottbusser Tor and Schlesischer Tor stations. What used to be the socialist east side of Berlin has come a long way towards catching up with the west. The Nikolai Quarter (not cheap) and the Gendarmenmarkt area are popular and appealing. If you're willing to travel a little, try Prenzlauer Berg (Schönhauser Allee and Husemannstrasse have a good selection of restaurants, many of them new).

Berlin is very much a late-night city, so you can put off your meal while you rest and freshen up; however, many restaurants do tend to fill up quickly so if you are fussy be sure to make a reservation.

If you are keen to try traditional German food (which can, incidentally, be very good value) why not try a pub meal? Vegetarians are also well catered for in Berlin, but it is advisable to use the specialist restaurants or those advertising international cuisine – picking from a German menu can be risky, as many dishes not specifying meat do in fact contain it hidden somewhere or other!

The variety of restaurants means that it is quite possible to eat cheaply – and if you're really short of money there's always the option of a kebab at any of the thousands of *imbiss* stands around the city. For a midday break, you can't beat the *Konditorei* (coffee and cake shop) – not cheap, but luxurious, regard it as a treat. Be aware when eating out that wine is quite expensive and tends to bump up the price of a meal in restaurants. Service and cover charges are generally included though it's customary to leave a tip with the waiter on payment (simply round up the price).

The following price guide indicates the price of an average meal per head, exclusive of drink. Remember that many restaurants classed as expensive can work out much cheaper if you do without wine.

★	up to €10
★★	€11–19
★★★	€20–29
★★★★	€30–45

German cuisine

Berliner Republik mit Brokers Bierbörse ★★★

Pleasantly informal, artfully decorated. Food specialities from all German federal states, augmented by nationwide choice of 15 draught beers.

Mitte, Schiffbauerdamm. Tel: (030)

30872 293. Open: daily 11.30am–4am. U-Bahn or S-Bahn to Friedrichstrasse.

Café am Neuen See ★★
Hearty Bavarian food, made complete with a lakeside beer garden (candlelit at night, with rowing-boat docks) in the green midst of the Tiergarten.
Tiergarten, Lichtensteinallee 2. Tel: (030) 254 4930. Open: daily 10am–11pm. U-Bahn to Hansa Platz or S-Bahn to Tiergarten.

Ermelerhaus ★★★★
A splendid rococo mansion dating from 1703. Plain German fare downstairs, more exclusive meals in the Wein-Restaurant upstairs.
Märkisches Ufer 10–12. Tel: (030) 279 3617. Open: daily 6pm–1am. U-Bahn to Märkisches Museum.

Feinkost Käfer Reichstag ★★★
Delectable *Deutscher* food and wine in the historic Reichstag's rooftop garden restaurant, right alongside the glass dome created by Sir Norman Foster. Dazzling views. Reservations advised.
Mitte, Platz der Republik. Tel: (030) 226 29933. Open: daily 9am–midnight. U-Bahn to Bundestag or S-Bahn to Unter den Linden.

Gastätte zur letzen Instanz ★★
All the woodsiness and kitsch you'd expect in an establishment that's been in business as a neighbourly *Kneipe* (pub and inn) since 1621. Genuinely local *Berlinerisch* specialities include fried and spiced *Buletten* (meatballs).
Mitte, Waisenstrasse 14–16. Tel: (030) 242 5528. Open: daily noon–1am. U-Bahn to Klosterstrasse or Alexanderplatz.

Heinrich ★★
Reservations are advisable at this popular establishment, originally the home of illustrator/cartoonist Heinrich Zille (*see p39*). Excellent south-German cuisine.
Sophie-Charlotten-Strasse 68. Tel: (030) 321 6517. Open: daily 4pm–1am. U-Bahn to Sophie-Charlotte-Platz.

Henne ★
Organically raised chicken is all that is served here, with cabbage or potato salad.
Kreuzberg, Leuschnerdamm 25. Tel: (030) 614 7730. U-Bahn to Kottbusser Tor.

Knese ★★
Simple Berlin cuisine, daily specials, excellent beers and fine wines.
Charlottenburg, Knesebeckstrasse 63. Tel (030) 884 130. Open daily 11am–1am. S-Bahn to Savignyplatz.

American

Hard Rock Cafe, Berlin HH ★★★
Typical American cuisine.
Meinekestrasse 21. Tel: (030) 884 620. Open: daily noon–2am. U-Bahn to Uhlandstrasse.

Jimmy's Diner ★★
Enjoy hamburgers and big portions till late in authentic décor.
Wilmersdorf, Pariser Strasse 41. Tel: (030) 882 3141. Open: Mon–Thur & Sun 11am–2am, Fri–Sat 11am–4am. U-Bahn to Hohenzollernplatz.

Austrian

Lutter & Wegner ★★★
A venerable wine-bar restaurant in business since 1811. Well known and critically praised for such traditional Austro-Germanic specialities as *Wiener Schnitzel* and *Tafelspitz*. Alongside the Gendarmenmarkt.
Mitte, Charlottenstrasse 56. Tel: (030) 202 9540. Open: daily 9am–2am. U-Bahn to Stadtmitte.

Chinese

Ho Lin Wah ★★★
A golden Buddha presides over this restaurant in the former Chinese Embassy.
Kurfürstendamm 218. Tel: (030) 882 1171. Open: daily noon–midnight. U-Bahn to Kurfürstendamm/ Uhlandstrasse.

French

Reste Fidèle ★★
Pleasant, warm surroundings, attentive service, good food.
Bleibtreustrasse 41. Tel: (030) 881 1605. Open: 11am–2am. U-Bahn to Savignyplatz.

Indian

Kashmir Palace ★★
Standard range of Indian food, done particularly well and critically praised. Convenient location close to the Zoologischer Garten and Kaiser Wilhelm Memorial Church.
Charlottenburg, Marburger Strasse 14. Tel: (030) 214 2840. Open: Mon 5pm–midnight, Tue–Fri noon–3pm & 6pm–midnight, Sat–Sun noon–midnight. U-Bahn to Bahnhof Zoo or Kurfürstendamm.

International cuisine

Alt-Luxemburg ★★★★
This traditional restaurant is in great demand. The chef, Karl Wannemacher, recommends the guinea-fowl. Reservations advised.
Windscheidstrasse 31. Tel: (030) 323 8730. Open: Tue–Sat 7–11pm. U-Bahn to Wilmersdorfer Strasse.

Borchardt ★★★
The Art Nouveau décor is the main attraction.
Französische Strasse 47. Tel: (030) 203 8711. Open: daily 11.30am–1am. U-Bahn to Stadtmitte. Kitchen closes at midnight.

Restauration 1900 ★★
Smart café-restaurant in Prenzlauer Berg (on the corner of Kollwitz-Platz) with an excellent reputation that is well deserved.
Husemannstrasse 1. Tel: (030) 442 2494. Open: daily 4pm–12.30am. U-Bahn to Sennefelder Platz.

Vox ★★★
In the Grand Hyatt Hotel in Potsdamer Platz. Stucco walls, parquet floors and dark oak furniture, plus a Japanese-style sushi bar and extra-large open kitchen. Sophisticated and cosmopolitan, with international clientele. A touch of history, too: Europe's first public radio broadcast was made from this site (the Vox-Haus studio) in 1923.
Mitte, Marlene-Dietrich-Platz 2. Tel: (030) 255 31772. Open: daily 6.30am–10pm. U-Bahn or S-Bahn to Potsdamer Platz.

Italian

Bar Centrale ★★
A busy establishment with trendy clientele and excellent food.
Yorckstrasse 82. Tel: (030) 786 2989. Open: 6pm–3am. U-Bahn to Yorckstrasse.

Die Schwarzenraben ★★
Blended retro and chic atmosphere in a former 19th-century *Kaffeehaus*; summertime dining on the garden terrace. An east-side neighbourhood favourite, happily rediscovered and reinvigorated since the fall of the Wall.
Mitte, Neue Schönhauser Strasse 13. Tel: (030) 283 91698. Open: daily 10am–1am. U-Bahn to Weinmeister Strasse or S-Bahn to Hackescher Markt.

Swiss

Restaurant Nola's am Weinberg ★★
An ideal setting for Swiss lunchtime specialities, served in a replicated mountain chalet nestled in the leafy Volkspark. Terrace dining in balmy weather is a bonus.
Prenzlauer Berg, Veteranen Strasse 9. Tel: (030) 440 40766. Open: daily 10am–1am. U-Bahn to Rosenthaler Platz.

Thai

Tuk-Tuk ★★
Comfortable atmosphere and authentic Thai–Indonesian cooking.
Grossgörschenstrasse 2. Tel: (030) 781 1588. Open: daily 5pm–1am. U-Bahn to Kleistpark.

Turkish

Bagdad ★
A popular restaurant; the garden is a plus.
Schlesische Strasse 2. Tel: (030) 612 6962. Open: daily 2pm–midnight. U-Bahn to Schlesisches Tor.

Istanbul ★★★
Well-established, not cheap but the food is authentic.
Knesebeckstrasse 77. Tel: (030) 883 2777. Open: daily noon–midnight. S-Bahn to Savignyplatz.

Merhaba ★★
Exotic and with genuine Turkish ambience; the food is reliable.
Wissmannstrasse 32. Tel: (030) 692 1713. Open: Mon–Sat 4pm–midnight. U-Bahn to Hermannstrasse.

Vegetarian/fish

Einhorn ★★
Amidst Schöneberg's busiest shopping crossroads, bountiful fast-food buffet selections include Moroccan specialities.
Schöneberg, Wittenbergplatz 5–6. Tel: (030) 218 6347. Open: Mon–Sat 11am–5pm. U-Bahn to Wittenbergplatz.

La Maskera ★★★
They even know what 'vegan' means, and the cuisine is Italian style.
Gustav-Müller-Strasse 1. Tel: (030) 784 1227. U-Bahn to Kleistpark.

Street cafés are always popular

The Berlin café

It was an Austrian, Johann Georg Kranzler, who introduced the delights of the coffee shop to grateful Berliners in 1825. So successful was his venture that within 40 years the café scene was as vibrant here as in Vienna or Budapest. This was the golden age of the Berlin coffee house. By now, the Café Kranzler, on the corner of Friedrichstrasse, had taken over the first floor of its original premises and had introduced a smoking saloon and outdoor tables. Guests – calling them customers would be too downmarket for this establishment – were offered mouthwatering *vol-au-vents* in a mushroom and cream sauce, followed by a light gateau, served with the obligatory topping of *Schlagsahne* (whipped cream). The porcelain dishes bearing the hallmark of the KPM factory were used and the cutlery was handcrafted silver.

Just across the street from the Kranzler was the even more prestigious Café Bauer, a palatial establishment decorated with gilded mirrors, marble-topped tables, chandeliers, and larger-than-life painted scenes from the lives of the Kaisers, attracting a clientele drawn almost exclusively from the aristocracy.

Café life spills on to the street in summer

The Café Möhring is a good place to stop for *Kaffee* and *Kuchen*

After World War I the focus of social life shifted towards the Ku'damm and the 'New West End'. The most famous establishment in this part of town was the Romanische Café, which once occupied the site of today's Europa-Center. Here one might encounter the novelist Thomas Mann, the famous opera star Richard Tauber, or the latest film idol hot out of the Babelsberg studios. Art and culture, rather than high society, was the meat of conversation here. If you weren't familiar with Expressionism or New Objectivity, better find somewhere else – perhaps the Telschow, where the pastry cook of the same name delighted in his speciality, the *Telschowschnitte*, a square pastry packed with successive layers of hard and soft chocolate with cream between each.

Those days have long gone, but the Berliner's love affair with the café remains undiminished. The Café Kranzler still exists, on the Ku'damm rather than Unter den Linden, and here visitors can still choose from an enticing selection of cakes and pastries: *Quark-Kirschkuchen* (cheesecake with fresh cherries), *Bienenstich* ('Bee-sting', with its distinctive flavour of almonds and butter icing), *Mokkatorte* (coffee gateau), *Apfelkuchen* (apple cake), *Erdbeertorte* (strawberry cake) – it would be cruel to go on.

The traditional time to come is about four in the afternoon, when Berliners take tea with their friends. There are the newspapers to read and matters to discuss, but, above all, the coffee house is a place to daydream, to off-load cares, and to slow down.

What to drink

Beer is the staple alcoholic drink in Berlin, much of it produced by the two large breweries: Schultheiss in Kreuzberg and Berliner Kindl in Prenzlauer Berg. Other German beers, as well as foreign varieties, are also in plentiful supply in pubs, especially in the trendier *Szene* (hang-outs) around Savignyplatz or out in Kreuzberg and Prenzlauer Berg.

Ask for *ein Bier* or *ein Pils* and you'll usually be presented with a glass of light draught beer (to be certain, ask for *Bier vom Fass*). If you want a bottle, ask for *eine Flasche*. In summer, *Berliner Weisse mit Schuss* appears on the menu. This is a low-alcohol beer sweetened with a dash of raspberry juice or *mit grün*, extract of green woodruff. Sometimes the waiter or waitress will bring the drink to your table when it has settled, but there's no hard-and-fast rule. Bars stay open all day and well into the night – until three or four in the morning in some places (Nollendorfplatz, for example) – though 1am is more common. Generally, pubs and cafés are extremely welcoming places, though the service in some Kreuzberg pubs can be a bit sullen – take this with a pinch of salt: it's a pose.

The historic Café Adler on Friedrichstrasse

Although Germany is famous as a wine-producing country, Berlin is not a wine-producing region. Most of the pubs in the centre of town double up as wine bars and, both here and in restaurants, there is a wide range of German and international wines. Popular German varieties include *Riesling* and *Sekt* (sparkling wine). If you want a dry wine ask for *trocken*; the word for sweet is *süss*. For those who don't like or don't want to drink alcohol, *ein Mineralwasser* will bring you a bottle of mineral water, usually carbonated. If you want it still, say *ohne Kohlensäure*.

Bars and cafés

Café Adler

This unpretentious Kreuzberg café, founded as an apothecary nearly two centuries ago, stood alongside Checkpoint Charlie (*see p102*) and housed American CIA spy-snooping quarters upstairs. Now customers come and soak up the old-time ambience. *Friedrichstrasse 206. Tel: (030) 251 8965. Open: Mon–Sat 10am–midnight, Sun 10am–7pm. U-Bahn to Kochstrasse.*

Café Kranzler

Berlin's most famous coffee house, with a tradition going back to the 19th

century. Terrace overlooking Ku'damm.
Kurfürstendamm 18–19.
Tel: (030) 887 1839.
Open: 8am–midnight. U-Bahn to Kurfürstendamm.

Café Savigny
Small café offering good breakfasts, filled baguettes and cakes. Tables outside in summer.
Charlottenburg, Grolmanstrasse 53–54.
Tel: (030) 312 8195.
Open: daily 10am–1am.
S-Bahn to Savignyplatz.

Café Wintergarten im Literaturhaus
Sunny winter garden and salon rooms. Breakfast, snacks and desserts.
Charlottenburg, Fasanenstrasse 23.
Tel: (030) 882 5414.
Open: Mon–Sat 9.30am–1am, Sun 9.30am–midnight.
U-Bahn to Uhlandstrasse.

Harry's New York Bar
Piano bar in the Hotel Esplanade.
Lützowufer 15.
Tel: (030) 254 78821.
Open: noon–3am. U-Bahn to Nollendorfplatz.

Josty
Post-reunification renaissance of a classy, two-level bar and café that thrived during Berlin's 'golden age' of nightlife in the 1920s.
Bellevuestrasse 1.
Tel: (030) 257 59702.
Open: Mon–Sat 9am–1am.
U-Bahn or S-Bahn to Potsdamer Platz.

Leydicke
Dating from 1877, this is one of the oldest *Kneipen* in Berlin. Justly famous.
Mansteinstrasse 4.
Tel: (030) 216 2973.
Open: Mon, Tue & Thur–Fri 4pm–midnight, Wed & Sat–Sun 11am–1am.
U-Bahn to Yorckstrasse.

Rote Harfe
Lively, atmospheric bar in Kreuzberg.
Heinrichplatz.
Tel: (030) 283 6877.
Open: 8am until late. U-Bahn to Hermannplatz.

Schwarzes Café
Long opening hours make this a popular haunt of nightclubbers.
Kantstrasse 148.
Tel: (030) 313 8038.
Open: 5pm–5am.
S-Bahn to Savignyplatz.

Turmstuben
Intimate, clubby and atmospheric; tucked inside the cupola atop the Französischer Dom.
Am Gendarmenmarkt.
Tel: (030) 204 4888.
Open: daily noon–1am. U-Bahn to Französische Strasse or Stadtmitte.

Wohnzimmer
Comfy sofas and kitschy knick-knacks.
Prenzlauer Berg, Lettesttrase 6.
Tel: (030) 445 5458.
Open: 10pm–4pm.
S-Bahn or U-Bahn to Schönhauser Allee.

Zeitlos
A 'beach bar' with bamboo décor, sandy floor and tropical cocktails.
Charlottenberg, Schlüterstrasse 60.
Tel. (030) 323 1681.
Open: 7pm–3am.
U-Bahn to Kurfürstendamm or Uhlandstrasse.

Zum Nussbaum
Warm and cosy but small. Originally 16th-century, the 'Walnut Tree' is in the Nikolaiviertel (Nikolai Quarter).
Propstrasse.
Tel: (030) 242 3095.
Open: noon–2am.
U-Bahn to Alexanderplatz.

The Berlin *Kneipe*

Every Berliner has his or her favourite pub – The Fat Lady, Beer Heaven, The Sturdy Dog, The Last Resort, Pig's Trotter Corner; for the inhabitants of this beer-loving and convivial city, the *Kneipe* is a home-from-home, a living room and a meeting point, a centre for gossip and diversion, a forum for discussion and for putting the world to rights. And there are plenty of pubs to choose from – more than 4,000 at the last count. But the traditional Berlin *Kneipe* is becoming something of an endangered species, especially in the more salubrious parts of the city. Dark forces are at work here in the insidious guise of changing tastes. Look for the tell-tale signs: brightly painted walls, smart chromium counters, no-smoking signs, foreign beers and – most pernicious of all – loud rock music.

Despite this worrying trend, the honest to goodness *Eck-Kneipe* (corner pub) can still be found in the old working-class neighbourhoods of Kreuzberg, Prenzlauer Berg and the Mitte. They can be identified by the brewery logo over the entrance (Berliner Kindl, Schultheiss), by the yellowing net curtains, the contented expression on the faces of the clientele and the ubiquitous billiard table. Heavy drinking, let's be honest,

There are around 1,300 breweries in Germany

The *Kneipe* – a favourite haunt for Berliners

is not uncommon here, alcoholism not unknown. But gone are the days, more than a century ago, when the Social Democratic Party had to appeal to its working-class members to 'abstain from alcohol' and turn instead to more dignified leisure pursuits. As the density of pubs in Berlin at that time was more than twice that of comparable industrial cities in Europe, it is perhaps not surprising that the appeal fell largely on deaf ears.

Today, as in the past, the *Kneipe* is a place of diehard custom and time-honoured tradition. Woe betide the drinker (ignorance can be no excuse) who ignores an invitation to clink glasses, or the visitor who inadvertently occupies the *Stammtisch*, the table reserved for regulars. Canny tipplers melt into the crowd by ordering a *Korn* (a light beer with a schnapps chaser) or a measure of the caraway seed liqueur called *Kümmel*.

Every *Kneipe* worth its salt serves the traditional local delicacies: Rollmops (pickled herring), *Solei* (pickled eggs), *Aal grün* (eel served in a dill or parsley sauce) and *Hackepeter* (a kind of meatloaf) – plain, no-nonsense fare.

Finally, a word of advice: visiting a *Kneipe* can be addictive – you have been warned!

Hotels and accommodation

There is no shortage of accommodation in Berlin – from luxury hotels to hotel-pensions and youth hostels – and the situation can only get better at the end of the current building boom. Furthermore, a surprisingly large number of hotels of every category are situated right in the heart of the city – no more than a few minutes' walk from the Ku'damm.

Most visitors to Berlin still prefer to stay in the western half. The east side suffers from a surfeit of hotels in the top price category, a hangover from the days when the government was anxious to relieve Western travellers of their hard currency. However, the situation has improved dramatically over the last ten years. Many new hotels have come up and others are being planned, while standards of service are also gradually improving.

Prices

Generally speaking, hotel prices are much the same as in other European capitals. The star ratings of former East Berlin hotels, however, should be taken with a pinch of salt – standards vary. The greatest variation is in hotels of the middle category.

Where Berlin scores highest is in the range and quantity of cheap accommodation. There are thousands of pensions, and not all are outside the central districts. Even if they are, remember that the public transport system is excellent.

The following is an indication of what one might expect to pay for a double room in a Berlin hotel. Breakfast is generally included in the price of accommodation, but it's best to check when booking.

★	up to €75
★★	€75–100
★★★	€100–150
★★★★	€150–200
★★★★★	€200 or above

Location

The greatest concentration of hotel accommodation of all types is around the Ku'damm and the more accessible parts of Charlottenburg. There are a number of large hotels in the Mitte district, almost uniformly expensive. Anyone wishing to stay in the historic heart of the city should bear in mind that the east side still offers very little in the way of nightlife, although some hotels do have high-quality restaurants. A great deal of lower-price accommodation is clustered in two central western districts, Schöneberg and Kreuzberg – the latter, in particular, will appeal to younger people. There is plenty of scope for anyone wishing to stay outside the city – in Wannsee, for example, or Grunewald – and not all the hotels there are expensive.

Booking

It should not be essential to book in advance, though to get the hotel of your choice it is advisable to plan ahead. Demand increases dramatically at certain times of the year – during the Berlin Film Festival at the end of February as well as throughout July and August. Many top hotels increase their rates when there are conferences on, so check carefully. For last-minute booking, see the agencies below, but remember that hotels claiming to be full do sometimes have rooms available when pressed.

Most hotels and pensions require a deposit and some insist on payment in full within a day or two of arrival.

Booking agencies in Berlin

Berlin Tourismus Marketing (BTM)
Tiergarten, Am Karlsbad 11.
Tel: (030) 250 025. www.btm.de
Information about available rooms and instant booking at: BTM-Office Tiergarten, *Budapester Strasse 45.*
www.berlin.realhotels.com provides information on accommodation as well.
For short-stay private accommodation, enquire at the Tourist Information Office on Budapester Strasse.

Berliner Zimmerreservierung Tiergarten
Budapester Strasse 50. Tel: (030) 283 861 67; fax: (030) 280 8057. www.berliner-zimmerreservierung.de

Freiraum
Arranges guest accommodation in houses and apartments.
Wiener Strasse 14. Tel: (030) 618 2008; fax: (030) 618 2006.
www.freiraum-berlin.com

Mitwohnzentrale
These agencies find private rooms and apartments for longer-stay guests, starting from one week.

WHERE TO STAY

Luxury hotels

Berlin has a number of top-class hotels with facilities to match. The newest, **Hotel de Rome** ★★★★★ (*tel: (030) 460 6090*), centrally situated on Bebelplatz, occupies what used to be the Dresdener Bank building. Also new, with 1,125 rooms making it the city's biggest hotel, **Estrel Berlin** ★★★★★ (*tel: (030) 68310*) is in the southeasterly Neukölln district. A multi-purpose layout includes a sizeable convention centre and theatre staging Las Vegas-type musical revues. Mitte's definitely deluxe **Regent Berlin** ★★★★★ overlooks the Gendarmenmarkt (*tel: (030) 368 03259*).

The **Grand Hotel Esplanade** ★★★★ (*tel: (030) 254 780*) is beautifully designed and not far from the

Tiergarten. This is not to be confused with the **Westin Grand Hotel** ★★★★ (*tel: (030) 20270*), another modern hotel occupying a prime site just off Unter den Linden. Another large hotel, with rooms overlooking the Kaiser-William Memorial Church, is the **Inter-Continental** ★★★★ (*tel: (030) 26020*).

Traditional hotels

Unfortunately, none of Berlin's magnificent pre-war hotels has survived. However, there are a number of modern establishments anxious to recapture past glories such as the **Bristol Kempinski** ★★★★ (*tel: (030) 883 340*), on the Ku'damm, descendant of the famous hotel that used to look out on Unter den Linden. The **Adlon** ★★★★ (*tel: (030) 226 111*) is another hotel with a famous name to live up to. The **Kronprinz** ★★★ (*tel: (030) 896 030*) is at the western end of the Ku'damm, and anyone wishing to sample the flavour of the 19th-century Mitte at a moderate price might like to stay in the **Charlottenhof** ★★★ (*tel: (030) 238 060*), right opposite the Gendarmenmarkt. **Riehmers Hofgarten** ★★★ (*tel: (030) 78098 800*) is a beautiful late 19th-century mansion situated in an attractive part of Kreuzberg.

Redevelopers did a superb job of converting a *c.* 1905 Wilhelminian manor house into the genteely elegant **Brandenburger Hof** ★★★★ (*Eislebener Strasse 14, tel: (030) 214 050*), an 82-room Relais & Châteaux property since 1991.

Designer hotels

Avant-garde furnishings (including bar stools designed by Philippe Starck and carpeting inspired by David Hockney)

The famous Hotel Adlon, built in 1907

embellish Charlottenburg's **Art Hotel Sorat Berlin** ★★★ (*Joachimstaler Strasse 29, tel: (030) 884 470*). Also art-filled to justify its name is trendy **art'otel berlin mitte** ★★★ (*Wallstrasse 70–73, tel: (030) 240 629*). Opened in September 2007, 167-room **Wall Street Park Plaza** ★★★★ (*Lietzenburger Strasse 85, tel: (030) 8877 770*) features Andy Warhol-influenced photographs by Christopher Makos and splashy interior décor by Beate Weller.

Out of town

There is a large choice of hotels in the suburbs or among the lakes and woods. The **Forsthaus Paulsborn** ★★★ (*tel: (030) 818 1910*) is a sedate period hotel and restaurant deep in the Grunewald forest. **The Belvedere** ★★★★ (*tel: (030) 826 0010*) is close to Grunewald yet not far from Charlottenburg and the Ku'damm. **Wannseeblick** ★★★ (*tel: (030) 80500 655*) has fine views across the lake, while the **Sorat Humboldt-Mühle** ★★★ (*tel: (030) 439 040*) occupies a converted industrial mill in Tegel which backs directly on to the water.

Pensions/budget hotels

There are literally hundreds of these. **Pension Kreuzberg** ★★ (*tel: (030) 251 1362*) is a favourite with students, while both the **Econtel Berlin** ★★ (*tel: (030) 34681 147*), near Schloss Charlottenburg, and **Hotel-Pension Wittelsbach** ★★ (*tel: (030) 864 9840, U-Bahn to Konstanzer Strasse*) cater for children. The central **Frauenhotel Artemisia** ★★ (*tel: (030) 873 8905*) is for women only.

Youth hostels

There are a number of youth hostels in Berlin. Bear in mind that if you stay out of town the curfew will preclude joining in the nightlife. The most central of all is
the **Jugendgästehaus am Zoo** ★ (*tel: (030) 312 9410*); next comes the **Jugendgästehaus am Kluckstrasse** ★ (*tel: (030) 261 1097*), not far from the Tiergarten. More remote are the **Jugendherberge Wannsee** ★ (*tel: (030) 803 2034*) and **Jugendherberge Ernst Reuter** ★ (*tel: (030) 404 1610*). You'll need an International Youth Hostel Federation card for most youth hostels.

Camping

Several decently clean campsites are located within Berlin's urban confines. Rates generally average €10 per person per night. Two are especially recommendable, offering showers and laundry facilities:

Landesverband DCC (Deutscher Camping Club), south of the Tiergarten in Schöneberg. *Geisbergerstrasse 11. Tel: (030) 218 6071. U-Bahn to Viktoria-Luise-Platz.*

Campingplatz Kohlhasenbrück, In the southwestern part of Berlin. Ten-minute walk from the nearest S-Bahn station. *Zehlendorf, Neue Kreis Strasse 36. Tel: (030) 805 1737. S-Bahn to Griebnitzsee.*

On business

Berlin's peculiar political status before 1989 practically disqualified it as a centre for international business. Today the situation is changing fast – investment levels in Berlin are unprecedented and the prospects have only got better since the German government moved here in 2000. Major international firms like Sony have already established their headquarters in the city. The local government is anxious to establish a reputation for Berlin as a centre for international conferences.

Business hours

Most businesses and government offices are open 9am–6pm Monday to Friday, though some open Saturday 9am–2pm. Banking hours are normally 9am–1pm and 2–6pm on weekdays, though they close at 5pm on Fridays. Most banks have extended hours on one or two days a week.

Chartered flights

Windrose Air

Flies private chartered flights to Berlin from destinations all over Europe. Also helps with hotel reservations, rented cars, theatre and restaurant bookings.
Tempelhofer Damm 1–7, 12101 Berlin. Tel: (030) 695 12400/12; fax: (030) 695 12404. www.windroseair.de

Conference centres and trade fairs

Hotel Steigenberger Berlin

An attractive modern hotel, centrally located. Siemens portable computers and software are available to guests on request.
Los-Angeles-Platz 1. Tel: (030) 212 70; fax: (030) 212 7117. www.berlin.steigenberger.de. U-Bahn to Kurfürstendamm.

Internationales Congress Centrum

This enormous space-age complex on the western fringes of the city opened in 1979. Facilities include 80 conference and meeting rooms, banqueting halls, banks, shops and restaurants.
Messedamm 22. Tel: (030) 30380. www.messe-berlin.com. Open: Mon–Fri noon–6pm, Sat 10am–2pm. U-Bahn to Kaiserdamm.

Inter-Continental Hotel Business Centre

A favourite base for German and international business men and women, the centre is equipped with computers, laser printers, desktop publishing facilities, photocopiers and portable telephones. One much appreciated feature is the excellent secretarial service. An interpreter service is also available.

The centre also has a number of executive suites, each provided with its own telephone number, outside line and fax.

The hotel can accommodate up to 1,250 conference participants. There is a direct bus service to and from the airport.

Budapester Strasse 2. Tel: (030) 26020; fax: (030) 260 22600. www.berlin.interconti.com. U-Bahn to Wittenbergplatz.

Mondial Hotel

The hotel's ideal location on the Kurfürstendamm and its relaxed atmosphere are its main advantages. Good conference facilities available.

Kurfürstendamm 47. Tel: (030) 884 110; fax: (030) 884 11150. www.hotel-mondial.com. U-Bahn to Uhlandstrasse.

Couriers

DHL

Overnight courier, international service. Last pick-up in city area at 4pm.

Forckenebkstrasse 9–13. Open: 9am–5.15pm. Tel: (030) 217 33906.

German language

German Language School

Special courses in business German.

Tel: (030) 780 0890. www.german-courses.com

Office stationery

Wolff & Matthes

Dederingstrasse 10. Tel: (030) 614 6088; fax: (030) 614 6020.

Other services

p'concept

Helps with the planning of conferences, sightseeing and hotel reservations.

Mitte, Kurfürstenstrasse 72–4. Tel: (030) 254 80670; fax: (030) 254 80671. www.pconcept.com

Bus-Verkehr-Berlin KG (BVB)

Organises sightseeing tours, makes hotel reservations and arranges trade fair programmes.

Grenzallee 15. Tel: (030) 683 8910.

No better place to do business – the Internationales Congress Centrum

Practical guide

Arriving

By air

All three Berlin airports are fairly near the city centre. The majority of international flights from Western Europe and the USA currently use Tegel Airport, which is about 8km (5 miles) to the northwest of the city and can be reached by bus or taxi. Increasing numbers of European flights arrive at Schönefeld, which is situated 20km (12 miles) southeast, and is directly accessible by S-Bahn and the DB German Rail's Airport Express service. Within the next few years, the airport will be renamed Brandenburg International (code BBI). Historic Tempelhof, established as a primarily military airport in 1923, now handles an increasingly limited number of domestic, charter and private-aircraft flights. About 15 minutes from downtown Berlin (*U-Bahn to Platz der Luftbrücke*), it is tentatively (and controversially) scheduled to close in the near future.

By rail

There are international train connections to Berlin from Paris, Brussels, Amsterdam, Copenhagen, Warsaw, Moscow, Vienna and Prague. The *Thomas Cook European Rail Timetable*, which is published monthly and gives up-to-date details of most rail services and many shipping services throughout Europe, will help you plan a rail journey to Germany. It is available online at *www.thomascookpublishing.com*, in the UK from some stations, from any branch of Thomas Cook, or you can call *01733 416 477*. In the USA, contact Rail Europe, *Westchester 1, 44 South Broadway, White Plains, NY 10601. Tel: 1-888-382-7245 (US); 1-800-361-7245 (Canada). www.raileurope.com*

Entry formalities

EC nationals must carry a valid passport or national identity card. Australian, Canadian, US and New Zealand nationals require a valid passport; all other nationals need a visa. Travellers who require visas should obtain them in their country of residence, as it may prove difficult to obtain them elsewhere.

Babysitters

Heinzelmännchen *Thielallee 38. Tel: (030) 831 6071.*
TUSMA *Hardenbergstrasse 35. Tel: (030) 315 9340.*

Berlin through the year

February Berlin International Film Festival.
March International Tourism Exchange.
May The Peace Race: cyclists from all over Eastern Europe.
10 May Writers gather in Bebelplatz to remember the 1933 book-burning.
July Jazz in July Festival; Love Parade (international techno festival).

September Berlin Arts Festival.
October Berlin Marathon (first Sunday) and the Berlin Motor Show.
3 October German Unity Day.
October, November Jazz Fest Berlin.
9 November Anniversary of the opening of the Wall for free movement.
31 December New Year celebrations at Brandenburg Gate.

Bicycles

Bicycles may be taken on the U-Bahn or S-Bahn: board at the doors with the relevant sign. You will need an *Ermässigungstarif* (reduced rate ticket). For bicycle hire *see pp160–61.*

Camping

Deutschen Camping-Clubs eV
The organisation runs three campsites on the outskirts of town which are clean, well-run and cheap. (*See also p177.*) *Lichtenbergerstrasse 27.*
Tel: (030) 249 7921.

Climate

See p6.

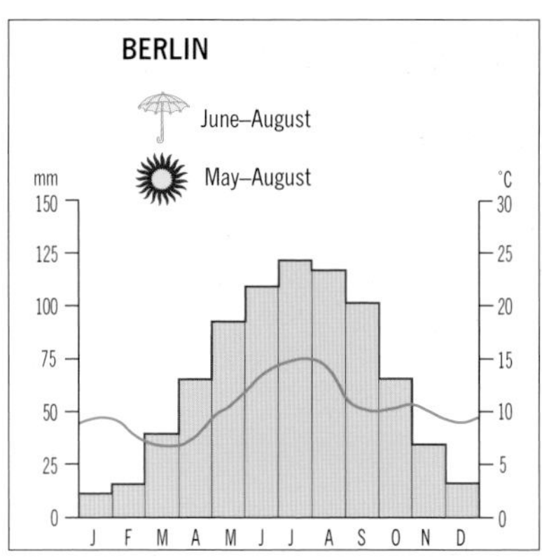

WEATHER CONVERSION CHART

25.4mm = 1 inch
°F = 1.8 × °C + 32

Conversion tables

See p183.
Clothes and shoe sizes in Berlin follow the standard sizes as in the rest of Europe.

Crime

Generally Berlin is a safe city, but visitors should take the usual precautions against thieves. Leave large amounts of money in the hotel safe, carry a money belt, take extra care in crowds and on the underground. While travelling at night be aware that lighting is poor on some streets. Make sure to report thefts and other crimes promptly to the police for insurance purposes.

Driving

A driving licence, national identity plate and vehicle registration certificate are required. Germans drive on the right. Speed limits are 130kmph (81mph) on motorways; 100kmph (62mph) on major roads; 50 kmph (31mph) in built-up areas. Fines for traffic offences are payable on the spot and police are empowered to remove car keys. It is illegal to drive after consuming alcohol and penalties are stiff.

Car rental

Hertz and other major firms operate from Tegel airport and major hotels.

Embassies and consulates

Australia *Wallstrasse 76–79, 10179 Berlin. Tel: (030) 880 088. www.australian-embassy.de*

Canada *IHZ Building, Friedrichstrasse 95, 10117 Berlin. Tel: (030) 20312. www.kanada-info.de*

UK *Wilhelmstrasse 70–71, 10117 Berlin. Tel: (030) 20457. www.britischebotschaft.de*

USA *Neustädtische Kirchstrasse 4/5 (Pariser Platz), 10017 Berlin. Tel: (030) 238 5174. www.usembassy.de*

Emergency telephone numbers

Police *110.*

Fire and Ambulance *112.*

Crisis Line In case of rape, contact the rape crisis line at *Stresemannstrasse 40. Tel: (030) 251 2828.*

Doctor (24-hour) *tel: (030) 310 031.*

Dentist (24-hour) *tel: (030) 89004.*

Health and insurance

There are no mandatory vaccination requirements and no vaccination recommendations other than to keep tetanus and polio immunisation up to date. As in every other part of the world, AIDS is present. *AIDS helpline: Berliner AIDS-Hilfe eV, Meinekestrasse 12. Tel: (030) 883 3017.*

Under an EU reciprocal arrangement, visitors from EU countries are entitled to medical treatment in Germany, but should obtain a European Health Insurance Card from their own National Social Security office. This should be presented to the doctor if possible before treatment or a consultation starts.

Claiming is often a laborious and lengthy process and you are only covered for medical care, not for emergency repatriation, holiday cancellation, and so on. You are therefore strongly advised to take out a travel insurance policy.

Library

The **British Council Library** (*Hackescher Markt 1, tel: (030) 311 099 48, open: Mon–Fri noon–6pm*) has an excellent range of books in English.

Lost property

Fundbüro der Polizei

Platz der Luftbrücke 6. Tel: (030) 699 36444.

BVG (public transport)

Potsdamer Strasse 182. Tel: (030) 256 23040. Open: Mon–Thur 9am–6pm, Fri 9am–2pm.

Media

Newspapers

There are several Berlin dailies: *Tagesspiegel* and *Berliner Morgenpost* are the main ones. Foreign-language newspapers are sold in stands and shops around Zoo station and the Ku'damm.

Internationale Presse Kiosk, *Hardenbergstrasse. Tel: (030) 881 7256. Open: daily 8am–midnight*, selling a variety of newspapers and periodicals.

Radio

BBC World Service – 90.2 FM.
Forces radios still exist on (British) BFBC 98.8FM and (American) AFN 87.9FM.

Money

The Euro (€) is the unit of currency used in Germany. There are seven denominations of the Euro note: 5, 10, 20, 50, 100, 200 and 500; eight denominations of coins: 1 cent, 2 cents, 5 cents, 10 cents, 20 cents, 50 cents and €1 and €2.

Exchange offices

Euro Change *Europa Center, Breitscheidplatz; tel: (030) 261 1484.*

Wechselstuben offering acceptable exchange rates can be found everywhere in Berlin. Friedrichstrasse Station is open 24 hours a day.

Major credit cards: American Express (*Friedrichstrasse 172, tel: (030) 201 7400*), Diners Club, MasterCard, VISA, EuroCard and JCB are acceptable, but cards are used less readily than in some other countries, so check first.

It is a good idea to take traveller's cheques, and those denominated in US dollars and other European currencies will be accepted. Hotel shops and some restaurants accept some kinds of traveller's cheque in lieu of cash.

National holidays

1 January New Year's Day
March/April, variable Good Friday, Easter Monday
1 May Labour Day

CONVERSION TABLE

FROM	TO	MULTIPLY BY
Inches	Centimetres	2.54
Feet	Metres	0.3048
Yards	Metres	0.9144
Miles	Kilometres	1.6090
Acres	Hectares	0.4047
Gallons	Litres	4.5460
Ounces	Grams	28.35
Pounds	Grams	453.6
Pounds	Kilograms	0.4536
Tons	Tonnes	1.0160

To convert back, for example from centimetres to inches, divide by the number in the third column.

MEN'S SUITS

UK	36	38	40	42	44	46	48
Rest of Europe	46	48	50	52	54	56	58
USA	36	38	40	42	44	46	48

DRESS SIZES

UK	8	10	12	14	16	18
France	36	38	40	42	44	46
Italy	38	40	42	44	46	48
Rest of Europe	34	36	38	40	42	44
USA	6	8	10	12	14	16

MEN'S SHIRTS

UK	14	14.5	15	15.5	16	16.5	17
Rest of Europe	36	37	38	39/40	41	42	43
USA	14	14.5	15	15.5	16	16.5	17

MEN'S SHOES

UK	7	7.5	8.5	9.5	10.5	11
Rest of Europe	41	42	43	44	45	46
USA	8	8.5	9.5	10.5	11.5	12

WOMEN'S SHOES

UK	4.5	5	5.5	6	6.5	7
Rest of Europe	38	38	39	39	40	41
USA	6	6.5	7	7.5	8	8.5

May, variable Ascension Day
May–June, variable Whit Monday
3 October German Unity Day
1 November All Saints' Day
25 December Christmas Day
26 December St Stephen's Day

Opening times

Banks
Banks are normally open Mon–Thur 9am–1pm & 2–6pm, Fri 9am–1pm & 2–5pm. The Berliner Bank at Tegel airport is open 8am–10pm.

Pharmacies (*Apotheke*)
These have late opening times, posted in the window or *tel: (030) 310 031* for information.
www.aponodie.de/be/Berlin
Europa-Apotheke (*Schnellerstrasse 21; tel: (030) 639 026 00*) is open Mon–Sat 8am–8pm.

Shops
See pp142–5.

Personal safety

Berlin is a non-violent city by and large, but visitors might do well to avoid the red-light district around Savignyplatz in Charlottenburg late at night. Employees of the U-Bahn will call a taxi for women travelling alone after 8pm.

Photo processing

Photo Huber (one-hour processing) at Europa-Center.
Tel: (030) 262 4666.

Post offices

Joachimsthaler Strasse 10 (near Zoo Bahnhof). Open: Mon–Sat 8am–midnight, Sun 10am–midnight.
S-Bahnhof Friedrichstrasse
Open: Mon–Fri 6am–10pm, Sat & Sun 8am–10pm.
Local post offices
Open: Mon–Fri 8am–6pm,
Sat 8am–noon.

Post boxes are bright yellow. Stamp machines can be found in central areas and outside post offices.

Public transport

See pp22–3. For information about all public transport in the Berlin area: **BVG-Pavillon**, Hardenbergplatz (Bahnhof Zoo). *Tel: (030) 194 49.* Open: daily 5.30am–10pm.

Train information – German National Railway (Deutsche Bahn)
Information Counter at Hauptbahnhof, Europaplatz. *Tel: (030) 194 49.*
Open: daily 6am–10pm.

Senior citizens

On presentation of an identity card senior citizens are entitled to half-price admission to museums and also to reductions on public transport, boat tickets, etc.

Student and youth travel

An International Student Identity Card (ISIC) entitles the holder to discounts at museums and some

Language

Knowledge of English is increasingly common in Berlin but an effort to speak German will be appreciated.

DAYS OF THE WEEK	
Monday	Montag
Tuesday	Dienstag
Wednesday	Mittwoch
Thursday	Donnerstag
Friday	Freitag
Saturday	Sonnabend/Samstag
Sunday	Sonntag

NUMBERS	
one	eins
two	zwei
three	drei
four	vier
five	fünf
six	sechs
seven	sieben
eight	acht
nine	neun
ten	zehn

Exotic drinks are on the menu at this downtown café

WORDS/PHRASES	
yes	ja
no	nein
please	bitte
thank you	danke
good morning	guten Morgen
good evening	guten Abend
good night	gute Nacht
small	klein
large	gross
quickly	schnell
cold	kalt
hot	warm
good	gut
room	Zimmer
menu	Speisekarte
breakfast	Frühstück
lunch	Mittagessen
dinner	Abendessen
white wine	Weisswein
red wine	Rotwein
bread	Brot
milk	Milch
water	Wasser
on the right	rechts
on the left	links
straight on	geradeaus
open	offen
closed	geschlossen
near	nähe
far	weit
how much	wieviel
expensive	teuer
cheap	billig
excuse me please	entschuldigen Sie bitte
do you speak English?	sprechen Sie Englisch?

theatres of up to 50 per cent. The publication *Berlin for Young People* is available from Tourist Information (*see* Youth hostels *p177*). For more information, visit *www.people-in-berlin.de.*

Sustainable tourism

Thomas Cook is a strong advocate of ethical and fairly traded tourism and believes that the travel experience should be as good for the places visited as it is for the people who visit them. That's why we firmly support The Travel Foundation, a charity that develops solutions to help improve and protect holiday destinations, their environment, traditions and culture. To find out what you can do to make a positive difference to the places you travel to and the people who live there, please visit *www.thetravelfoundation.org.uk*

Taxis

Zentraler Taxi-Ruf,
tel: 0800 800 222 3000 or *222 2255*.
For chauffeur service,
tel: (030) 456 1111.

Telephones

Many public phone boxes are marked *Kartentelefon* and are operated by phonecards (sold at post offices). Booths marked International or telephones in post offices are for long-distance calls. The code for Berlin from abroad is IDD+*30*.

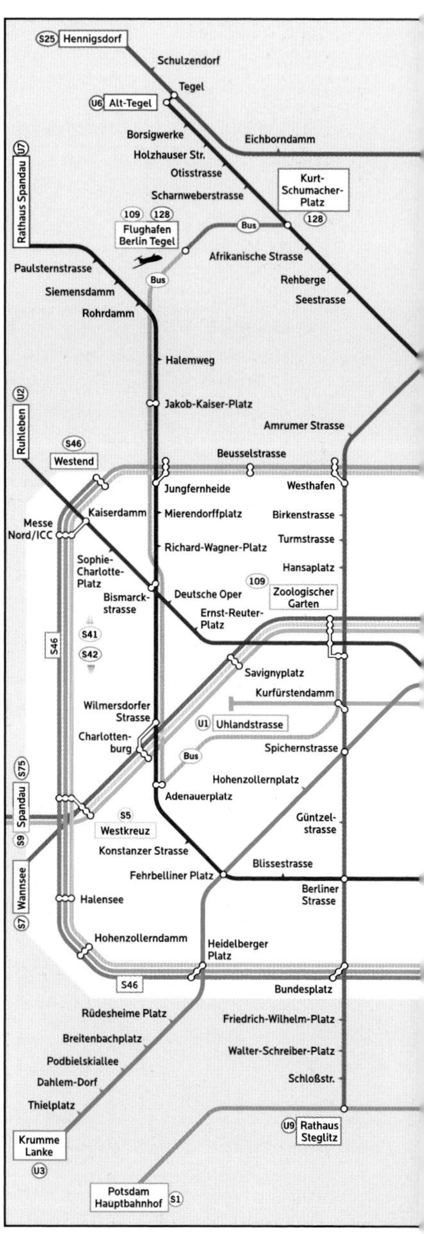

U-Bahn and S-Bahn

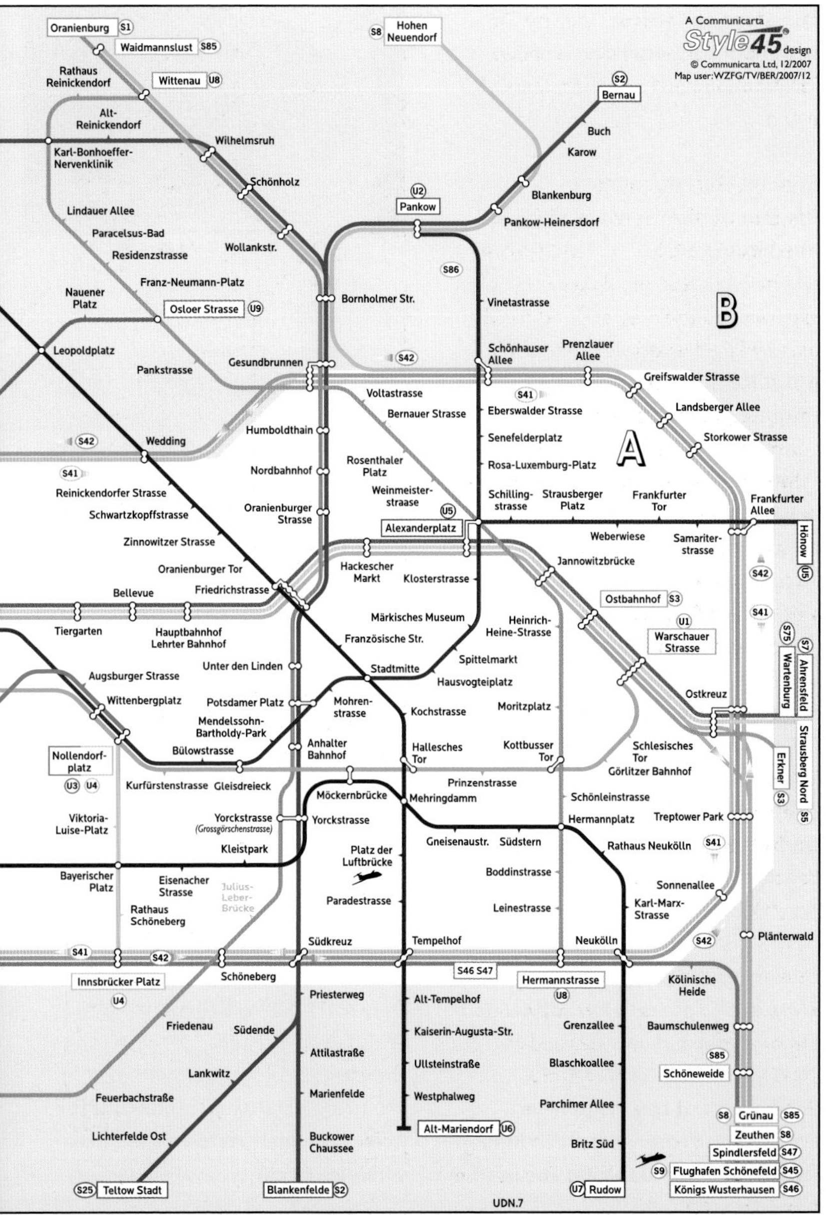

Operator *03*
International Operator *0010*
Directory Enquiries *11833*
International Enquiries *11837*
Telegrams *01805 121210*

Time

Berlin is one hour ahead of GMT in the winter and two hours ahead in the summer.

Tipping

Service charges are included in prices but it is customary to round up the bill.

Toilets

Most public toilets cost €1.
Men – *Herren*;
Women – *Damen* or *Frauen*.

Tourist information

Berlin Tourismus Marketing (BTM) *Tiergarten, Am Karlsbad 11. Tel: (reservation) (030) 250 025, (general information) 0190 016316, (foreign calls (0049) 700 862 37546).*

Berlin Tourist Info
Tel: 565 5500 566 7840 (for reservations).

BTM Office Tiergarten
Budapester Strasse 45 (information about available rooms and instant booking; no telephone). Open: Mon–Sat 10am–7pm, Sun 10am–6pm.

For private accommodation and apartments, **Zimmervermittlung Dentler**. *Tel: (030) 56555 111. www.berlin-bed.com*

Sunset on Bismarckstrasse

Berlin on the Internet
The following sites are useful: *www.btm.de* (general information); *www.berlin.de* (general information); and *www.smb.spk-berlin.de* (museums).

Tourist offices
UK *PO Box 2695, London W1A 3TN. Tel: (020) 7317 0908. www.germany-tourism.de*
USA *122 East 42nd Street, 52nd Floor New York, NY 10168-0072. Tel: (212) 661 7200. www.cometogermany.com*

Travellers with disabilities

Berlin is wheelchair friendly – buses have rear-door access and safety straps for wheelchairs. For help with renting wheelchairs and other problems or for information contact:
Deutscher Paritätischer Wohlfahrtsverband, *Brandenburgischestrasse 80. Tel: (030) 860 010*; or **Landesamt für Zentrale Soziale Aufgaben, Landesversorgungsamt**, *Gustav-Meyer-Allee 25. Tel: (030) 464 2056.*

Index

Acknowledgements

Thomas Cook wishes to thank the photographers, picture libraries and other organisations for the loan of the photographs reproduced in this book, to whom copyright in the photographs belongs.

ALAMY IMAGES/Content Mine International 153
TOM BROSS 19, 27, 86, 87, 145, 155, 168, 170
DREAMSTIME/Jan Kranendonk 22, Timehacker 150
FLICKR/freakyman 15, Frank B Daugaard 24, dff 29, Manamanah 34, Wordridden 48, handtwist 52, mediaman // 58, Torchondo 64, Seier+Seier+Seier 67, aerogon76 90, Doratagold 137, James Cridland 173, peterthefat 176
CHRISTOPHER HOLT 11, 26, 38, 43, 46, 47, 53, 60, 71, 80, 100, 119, 122, 126, 127, 134, 140, 141, 147, 152, 161, 163
MARY EVANS PICTURE LIBRARY 131
PICTURES COLOUR LIBRARY 45, 93, 116
SPECTRUM COLOUR LIBRARY 4, 7, 10, 25, 35, 113
THOMAS COOK PUBLISHING 31
WIKIMEDIA COMMONS/Jim Hood 28, Gryffindor 63, James G Howes 138
WORLD PICTURES/PHOTOSHOT 1, 57, 109, 143, 157, 167

The remaining pictures are held in the AA PHOTO LIBRARY and were taken by: ANTONY SOUTER 14, 23, 44, 50, 51, 54, 55, 56, 78, 89, 101, 115, 117, 123, 124, 125, 135, 149, 154, 179, 185, 188
ADRIAN BAKER 5, 17, 37, 59, 74, 81, 83, 84, 133, 169
DOUG TRAVERSO 128, 129, 172

For CAMBRIDGE PUBLISHING MANAGEMENT LTD:
Project editor: Rosalind Munro
Typesetter: Trevor Double
Proofreader: Karolin Thomas
Indexer: Karolin Thomas

SEND YOUR THOUGHTS TO
BOOKS@THOMASCOOK.COM

We're committed to providing the very best up-to-date information in our travel guides and constantly strive to make them as useful as they can be. You can help us to improve future editions by letting us have your feedback. If you've made a wonderful discovery on your travels that we don't already feature, if you'd like to inform us about recent changes to anything that we do include, or if you simply want to let us know your thoughts about this guidebook and how we can make it even better – we'd love to hear from you.

Send us ideas, discoveries and recommendations today and then look out for your valuable input in the next edition of this title.

Emails to the above address, or letters to Travellers Series Editor, Thomas Cook Publishing, PO Box 227, Coningsby Road, Peterborough PE3 8SB, UK.

Please don't forget to let us know which title your feedback refers to!